MUSIC AND LANGUAGE WITH
YOUNG CHILDREN

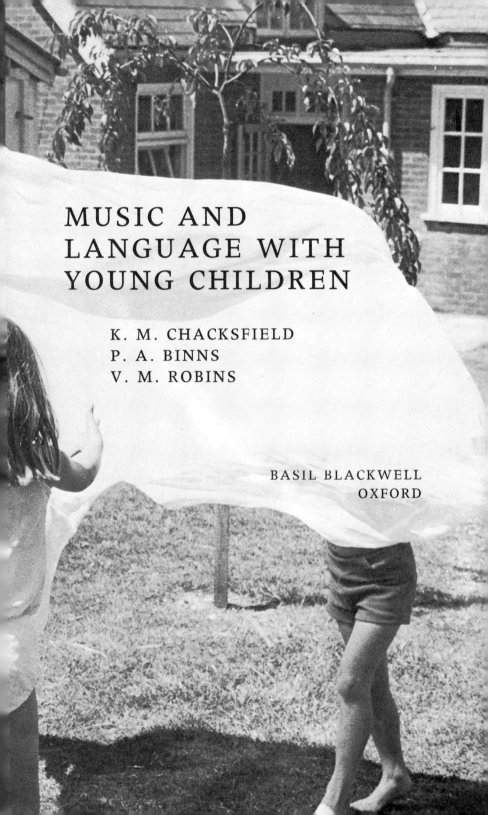

MUSIC AND
LANGUAGE WITH
YOUNG CHILDREN

K. M. CHACKSFIELD
P. A. BINNS
V. M. ROBINS

BASIL BLACKWELL
OXFORD

TEXT FIGURE DRAWING BY NICHOLAS ROUS
PHOTOGRAPHY BY GILES WOODFORDE

Printed in Great Britain by BAS Printers Limited, Wallop, Hampshire

Contents

Preface and Acknowledgements

This Group 4 Infant School, where the interest and development in Music and Language described in this book is continuing, is situated in a middle-class area which lies between Southampton and Winchester, within reach of the Isle of Wight, the South Coast and the New Forest.

The premises consist of a central brick building erected in 1908, containing three classrooms and administrative offices; there are a further five temporary classrooms and a wartime dining-room and kitchen across the playground. Two more classes are housed in the Annexe in purpose-built classrooms down a side-road about 200 yards from the school.

When this book was written there were six classes where children were grouped from 4 + to 6 years of age and four classes from 6 to 8 years old.

We would particularly like to thank all the following members of the teaching staff who, by their interest and co operation, have helped in the successful development of the ideas which this book attempts to set forth: Mrs. V. Olds, Deputy Headmistress, Mrs. A. Gebbie, Mrs. B. Whatley, Mrs. D. Ashford, Mrs. M. Watts, Mrs. E. Ewens, Mrs. V. York, Mrs. V. Eminton, and Mrs. A. Powell.

Members of the Advisory Service of the Hampshire Education Authority have been most helpful, and we are especially grateful to Mr. R. Fletcher, G.R.S.M., A.R.M.C.M., County Music Adviser, Mr. R. James, Senior Adviser for Speech and Drama, Mr. P. Williams, Adviser for Speech and Drama, and Miss N. M. Millington, Physical Education Adviser. We are also grateful to Mr. G. Self of La Sainte Union College of Education for the use of a synthesiser.

The advice and encouragement from the Department of

Education and Science through their Area Training Organisation Courses have been invaluable.

We are most grateful to Mr. R. A. Chacksfield, Headmaster of Highcliffe County Junior School, and Mr. B. Sprague, Deputy Headmaster of Weeke County Junior School, and particularly appreciative of the invaluable criticism and practical help in the making of this book given by Mr. J. Cutforth and Mrs. G. Taylor. We are grateful too, to Mrs. P. Bosier for her ever-ready help in typing the manuscript.

K. Merle Chacksfield
Headmistress, Chandler's Ford
County Infant School
P. A. Binns
V. M. Robins

December 1973

CHAPTER 1

The First Steps in Music

When I was a probationary teacher, tackling a reception class in an infant school for the first time, my Headmistress asked me: "What can you do in the musical field with your class?" I told her that I had started to learn the recorder but, other than that, could not "do music". Then I brightly added, "But I shall work with them on sounds, on listening and with home-made instruments, which could prepare them for creative English and phonic work." In retrospect, I realise the falseness of this distinction, since now I can say that music is an integral part of my classroom work, giving original and creative results which centre on musical principles. I have been helped in the exploration of these principles by my Headmistress, our music consultant, County Advisors and by attending a course for one day on Movement and Drama, which was very useful indeed.

When I began, I looked forward to working with the music consultant on the staff; she has a music room, but also collaborates with each teacher in the classrooms. Fortunately neither she, our Headmistress nor I believed that "music is the responsibility of one teacher in the school, who teaches it more happily than anyone else".[1] If this viewpoint were implemented, it would close the world of music to most children in the school, leaving only a few lucky ones to be fitted into the precious hours of the Music Room.

I started by arranging one of the bays in the reception room as a music area, with a varied collection of sound-producing materials, including junk which could be shaken, stirred, hit, or touched in any way to make a sound. The children added to this area by bringing such things as coffee tins half filled with rice or a biscuit tin with elastic bands of different thicknesses stretched across it. They also made an assortment of shakers in the class-

1

room, filling containers such as tins and plastic bottles with peas, nails, macaroni, etc. and decorating them with papier mâché.

Apart from this bay we used an area in the corridor outside where a few children could work with instruments such as drums, glockenspiels and chime bars. During the first half of the term, the children in both these areas explored the various possibilities of sound, and I used* some of their home-made instruments in movement sessions.

It was the Headmistress who suggested that the children could write down their sounds. As I only had a first-term intake of 15 children, I decided to experiment with all of them. Giving them each a long piece of paper and a thick crayon, I took a squeezy bottle filled with dried peas, shook it and asked them to listen. Then I suggested that they write down the sound in any way they liked. Not one child asked "How?" or "What do I do?"; The results varied from

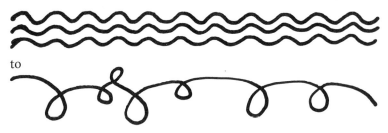

to

All had noticed, consciously or not, the continuous even nature of the sound. I then held a suspended six-inch nail and hit it, at regular intervals, with another nail. Again the children wrote down the sound unhesitatingly as

or as

and one boy wrote

        spot   spot   spot   spot

Copying among the fifteen children was reduced to a minimum, since they were spread around a large classroom, some on the floor, others on work surfaces of different heights. The children were able to write down the sounds at second hand, as it were, since they had all used these "instruments". They could

2

also read and play the sounds back, even after a lapse of a week or so.

I noticed that their marks on the paper were often an extension of the arm or hand movement used to make the sound. A wooden beater, lightly flicked on a tin, would often be written down as

and this is surely more meaningful to the child involved than the teacher writing down

for him.

To explore the link between sounds and the movement of the body, I asked the children to shape their mouths, make a sound and to write it down. Lips in a circle gave the sound *ooh, ooh, ooh,* and they used as a symbol the shape of the mouth:

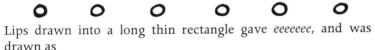

Lips drawn into a long thin rectangle gave *eeeeeee,* and was drawn as

and then, as the child experimented with the dynamics of the sound, changed to

One boy equated loudness with thickness of line, so that his *eeeeee* sound, which started quietly, became louder and then quieter, was written down as

It was also interesting that a child would see sound in different sizes, so that the girl who had begun with

changed it to

o o o o o o

when she made the sound louder and louder.

The children's aural discrimination was developed by, perhaps, listening to sounds outside the room, followed by a discussion on which they thought were harsh and loud, which soft, quiet and delicate. At such times, if the child attempted to imitate a sound such as a clock, personal interpretation was encouraged. If "tick, tock" was offered—which actually seldom happened—I asked the group to listen carefully and see what other kind of sounds they could hear in the clock. The more conventional sound imitations, such as "pitter, patter" for rain, were not rejected; they were praised, but more were asked for. Children often do not hear the adult's idea of a sound, but they frequently discover a far more accurate vocal imitation of it.

This point can be illustrated by a frieze on which the reception class worked in the spring term. There had been much rain, so a group started painting, crayonning, and using collage for people with umbrellas or big rain hats, and these were grouped together on a large frieze background. Looking at it made me think of the sound of rain and the many ways in which water falls and moves, and I decided on an experiment. I brought the group together in front of the frieze and asked how they could show rain apart from painting it. I suggested that they close their eyes, imagine rain and listen to it. Was it soft, light rain or a pouring, heavy thunder rain? (It was unfortunately a brilliant sunny day!) I asked for the sounds their rain made, and was immediately told not "splish, splosh", but *pt pt pt* and *plit, plot*. One child gave *zzzz* for more persistent rain, and a lightning crack was *tsing*. The group suggested that I write down their sounds for the rain, and gradually the picture was covered by these symbols, the size of which represented the intensity of the sound.

4

 were thunder

claps, and

pt pt
  pt pt   small rain drops dancing up and down on an umbrella.
   pt

I again noticed the accompanying movement which seems such an integral part of music work at this age. When the rain was *pt pt* a flicky movement of finger and thumb was made, and when the child shouted *CRICK*, his arm struck down in a quick, direct stab. The class of 27 enjoyed "singing" this frieze. With their voices as instruments, as I pointed first to the quieter rain sounds and then to the heavier thunderstorm, they brought the storm from the shops round the corner, up the road and into the classroom, where it erupted in full force!

By now, while watching and working with the children, I had begun to realise that music, especially at this developmental stage, is about being sensitive to sounds, about saying things through sounds, and, particularly for infant children, about listening to sounds that have never been heard before. It is small wonder, therefore, that the child will wish to find his own way of putting on paper his own most personal expression and excitement. Percussion work, nursery rhymes, correct breathing and diction for singing, sol-fa and traditional notation are still important, but obviously these techniques must not limit the child's musical world. But in case any of the children thought that music is only written in black and white notes on five lines, I made a chart to reinforce their symbols as a valid method of music writing.

During this first year, I had realised, through working with the music consultant, that one of the things to encourage the child to aim for, as his exploration of sound developed, was a pattern or shape to his sounds.

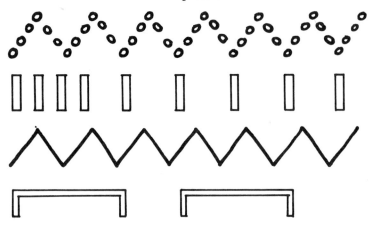

you can sing a
sound pattern

Explorations in sound

In my second year, I had a class of 30 children—35 after January
—all of whom would be six during that school year. Now the
music area also contained various bottles, holding different levels
of liquid. These could make sounds if struck, shaken or blown
into. Since the class was new to me, I let them explore this area
on their own, to show that anything, treated in any way, can
make a sound for music.

I experimented with putting down the children's own sounds,
but also tried to set down the sounds of a record they particularly
liked. Various classes had been working on Colour, and our
class had taken this as "Colour in Animals". The children had
heard Saint Saëns's *Carnival of the Animals* in the music room,
and were very excited by the instruments making animal noises.
I gave each of them a piece of paper and asked them to listen,
and put down the sounds they heard. Again not one child asked
what I meant, although some children had come from other
schools and had not met this activity before. The lion's roar
was recorded as

6

and as

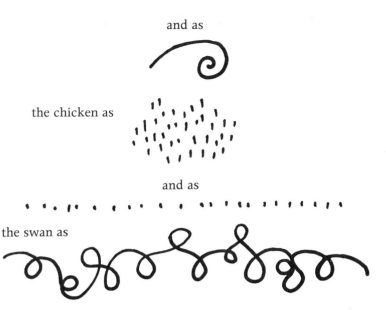

the chicken as

and as

the swan as

When doing this, the children's echoing movement was particularly striking. When the chickens pecked, the children's bodies were tight and tense, their writing hand pecking and snapping at the paper. When they put down the swan's fluid and continuous music, their arms, head and necks mirrored the movement of the sound, and the crayon acted as an extension of the sounds which were filling the air and travelling through the child on to the paper.

It is difficult to gauge exactly how much other activities benefit and are heightened by the child's developing sensitivity to aural perception. Who can tell if the children's handling of rhythm and feeling for balance and alliteration in the following poem, was developed by their previous work on sounds?

Colour the Animals

Sometimes you see a white swan in the sky,
I like to see it glide and fly.
Sometimes you see aeroplanes and you forget
What shape it is and you let
Your brains forget, and you think it's the swan.

7

There is yellow gold which sparkles in the deer,
It shines, glitters like a diamond,
And like bubbles in ginger beer,
And like gold treasure on an island.

A chicken is yellow and it's got a red comb,
A comb the colour of blood and red crayon.
Feathers like yellow flowers they gave to the sun god in Rome,
Feathers like raw, uncooked red meat on the bone.

*(Completely written by a class of 30 children, average age 5 years
7 months)*

The work on the *Carnival of the Animals* was extended into a carnival of people from different countries. Again it is very possible that the aural training had helped the children's ears and minds to become attuned to which syllables were suitable, which would be juxtaposed, and to the final choice of names. The Negro on the frieze was called *Calikobompeeshando*; the Jamaican, *Happy Muleeds*; the Eskimo *Pelose*; the Indian *Rambadar*; the Red Indian *Genimo*; and the Chinese was named *Chi Nee Chee*.

In the second term the music area was extended, since the children had begun to understand and analyse duration, pitch, tempo, the dynamics, mood and style of sounds and sound patterns, and would not be confused by more material. It contained objects which could all be touched in different ways: hit, plucked, shaken or made to sound in any way the children could think of. There were nails of various lengths, which made different sounds when hit, and wood shavings suspended from the ceiling; a three-foot-wide section of a tree; an enamel bowl; a home-made chordal dulcimer; corrugated cardboard; beaters of wood, metal, plastic; paintbrushes; different lengths of old rulers joined together with string to make a shaker; a yoghurt pot containing screws, nuts, nails, bolts; and tissue paper and silver foil pinned on the wall. Pitch charts were made, and used to reinforce "high" and "low" concepts. One chart showed butterflies high above the flowers, with worms lying in the depths of the earth. The children devised sounds appropriately pitched for the butterflies and the worms. Another chart showed three children of different heights holding hot cross buns. The buns were drawn so that the child's eye movement mirrored his voice direction when he sang:

Hot   *buns*
     cross

Later that term the children made a bird-frieze on which each bird was made with a different material. They gave sounds to the birds, making sure that these were related to the shape, size or material of each. The little bird, made of collage, was given a "rustling, papery sound", *pprr, pprr, pprr*. The silver-foil bird said *tling, mling, tling, mling*. This was set down both with words and with these symbols

since "mling" was a higher sound than "tling".

This Birds topic led to the making of models of "Say Birds", taken from a B.B.C. television phonic series, which had bird characters, imprinted with a letter of the alphabet; they were used to provide letters when needed. If, for instance, bananas and baked beans were wanted, the *b* "Say Bird" spoke, producing a string of *b*'s which could be used to make up the word. When the children had made *b* and *s* "Say Birds", they explored the possibilities of the sounds which each one made, using their voices as instruments. When they made a sound pattern of different length *b*'s, some exploded, some were quiet and then intensified. They also chose two poems which they thought were particularly appropriate to the individual "Say-Birds". Their grasp of the "colour" of sounds was shown by the realisation that the *b* "say-bird" could be suitably described by phrases of the poem, *The Bugle Billed Bazoo* by John Ciardi, where a "bugle-beaked bazoo" "shrieks and scolds the whole day through". The children noticed that an *s* sound is much lighter, more sibilant and more mysterious than *b* and so chose the following

9

lines of *Half Awake* by Frances Cornford for their *s* "Say-Bird":

> There is a bird, they say,
> that only sings when snow is on the way,
> and the moon ice cold.
> His name is so old,
> that now his name is lost.
> But I have heard
> his nest is made of frost.

This feeling for the "colours" or tones of sound is very evident in the children's musical explorations. It appeared again in music created for an assembly on Colour, using Oscar Wilde's story, *The Happy Prince*. To highlight this story, the children made "golden" and "leaden" music, for the "before" and "after" stages of the Prince's statue. For the "golden" music, the children chose light, delicate sounds, by striking a cymbal, shaking Indian bells, and rattling milk bottle tops. Having worked out the sound sequence, the children decided it needed repeating to emphasise the sound pattern. It was then put down on paper and used as a score in the assembly. The "golden" score was recorded in red, yellow and orange:

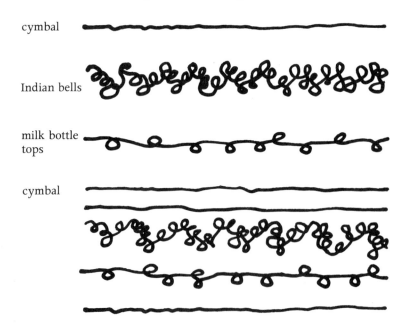

It seemed to the Headmistress, the music teacher and me in discussion that anything and everything can be used by the child of first school age in order to express his ideas in music. This was proved when the children, working on the theme of time, were preparing an assembly on The Future. They wanted to make some music which reflected the fears they had expressed on this topic, as shown in the following poem:

Time When Monsters Grow

There may be monsters up in space,
and a black crow with them.
There may be people up in space
and there could be birds with them.
Cracks will come and blow up the moon,
and the scared people fall down,
float down floppy through the black dark.
Follow what you find in space
and you may destroy history.

The children first made a collection of sound effects, using anything around them, from a controlled, measured scraping and flicking on the mat, an oscillating, breathy, *ooh ooh ooohh ooh* with the voice, to a final clash on the gong. This brought the whole pattern to a crescendo, when the varying pitch and cumulative effect had built up a feeling of suspense and gathering fear. They had to adapt the writing down of the score to show that the "music of the future" began with the scraping on the mat and the other sounds were brought in one by one. It was first written as if all the sounds began simultaneously, and then, having been asked if they thought it satisfactory, the children realised that the score should mirror the cumulative effect. This was the result.

fingers scraping on the mat

vocal effects

cymbals

tapping sticks

'ooh' vocal

rattling on drum

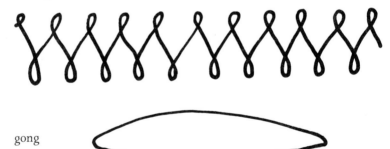

gong

During all these activities, and especially in the work on the *Music of the Future*, the children showed that music is finding ways of building with various combinations and textures of sounds.

12

The structuring of the music area in the classroom, with its collection of junk material, has been questioned because the musical potential of tins and bottles is limited, thus confining the child's development.[2] This viewpoint seems to imply that creative music work is something for the "un-musical", while "the real thing" is left to those who can play an instrument and deal with crotchets and quavers. Many books on Primary music do not seem to recognise that the raw materials of music—sounds—are basically very simple, and that these materials can be explored and formed into musical ideas. We found that the young child began by finding out what he could do with the basic material. He did not work by rules, nor did we expect him to conform to musical convention. We trusted him with enough integrity to shape the material to fit the ideas which he had imagined.

When using unorthodox sound-producing materials—including junk—we try to draw from the child his own ideas, helping him to express them in his own way. We do not expect him to follow traditional melodic shapes and harmonies which, to us, accord with "agreed" principles. We do not impose on him at this stage of his development our expectations of what "music" should be. We noticed that he automatically thought it right to use, as Debussy said, "any sounds in any combination". Because of this, the child begins to understand the varied ways in which these sounds can be built into patterns.

The education of the child's "feeling" and sensitivity needs as much attention as other techniques and skills. Indeed it should be developed first as John Paynter points out, "because without it other skills will be empty and of little value".[3] If the sounds made by children in a classroom are to become music, this may not only be achieved by using older musical techniques. Those who have learnt to listen with sensitivity try things out and evolve their own techniques; they also become aware of already established ones to interpret their ideas. They find ways of controlling and reproducing sounds, and begin to select specific sounds and to construct patterns.

We try not to impose traditionally developed expectations on children, since if they are freely trusted to explore sounds, they will produce exciting, truly creative patterns. These have a very definite sense of style, which is often different from the expected one. Children's sound patterns are often strongly influenced by the time factor and tone-colour, rather than by melody, and the results sound more akin to Berio or to African drum music than to melodic eighteenth-century compositions. The teacher must not judge hastily, saying that it is wrong; it is simply different in style. The very young child does not usually balance these three elements of musical style, but focuses on one or two, choosing their possibilities with great concentration, as can be seen in the following example.

John was working in the music area. He first collected a series of sounds, and then listened carefully as he played each one, writing it down quickly afterwards. He then played the whole sound pattern through, reading it off his own score.

Hitting a six-inch nail suspended from the ceiling on a cord:

O　　O　　O　　O　　O　　O　　O　　O

Fingers continuously playing over the strings of chordal dulcimer:

Strings of chordal dulcimer struck once with wooden beater and then a six-inch nail struck with same beater:

Continuous shaking of tin-foil milk bottle tops threaded on cotton:

Voice used as instrument to make hard explosive *g* sound, which rose and fell in pitch:

g ᵍ g g ᵍᵍ g ᵍ ₉₉₉ᵍᵍ₉

14

Irregular beats on enamel bowl with paintbrush:

A soft continuous "swishing" over base of bowl with the bristles of a brush:

The child who explores junk material can build up a collection of sound effects, and organise them into an order that satisfies the ear and keeps him interested. He often sees the need for another child or two to make other sounds to extend the sound pattern; and for a conductor, who is there not to beat time in the usual way, but to mark the moment when the next event should begin. The teacher may sometimes help him to see that too many sounds could get in the way, for to limit the sounds available makes the child get as much out of his material as possible. By careful questioning, she may lead him towards changing the volume and intensity, ensuring that he is listening acutely as well as executing his sounds.

Making such music offers everyone a chance to do something musically creative; it has its own disciplines and demands as much sensitivity to shape and texture as does more traditional composition. None of these musical activities is undisciplined, and although excitement and a sense of adventure are very evident in a group working in this way, so too are precision and a wish to understand what is happening in the music. Allowing the child to work with his own time intervals, and with his own kinds and "colours" of sound ensures that he is not frightened or restricted, as can happen with conventional music techniques. The child will simply be concentrating on a form of expression personal and meaningful to him or the group involved.

References

1. M. Brearley (Ed.), *Fundamentals in the First School*, p. 129, Blackwell, 1970.
2. *Op. cit.*, p. 127.
3. J. Paynter, *Hear and Now*, Universal edition, 1972, p. 11.

15

CHAPTER 2

Exploring Sounds

We live in an age of sound pollution when our environment is disturbed by constant noise, our ears violated by aircraft taking off, road drills and the shattering racket of motor cycles. In many homes the radio is never switched off, although no-one listens to it. Even when sound is not obtrusive, it exists in the form of what has been aptly described as "aural wallpaper", such as background music in supermarkets. We cannot protect our children from this pollution, but we should try to help them to become selective in their listening, to train their ears to be discriminating, to become aware of new sounds and by the development of their memories. We might, for example, use this simple approach to five- and six-year-olds.

"Close your eyes and think hard of your Mother's voice when she comes into your bedroom to say, 'Good morning', or when she sings to you or tells you a story."

After a pause we said, "Now, open your eyes. Do you remember what your Mother's voice sounds like?"

"Yes," answered the children.

One boy said, "My Dad gets me up!"

"Do you remember your Dad's voice?"

"Yes," to general deep gruff voices from the children.

"Have you a baby at home? Do you remember the sounds he makes?"

The children seemed to recall the sound of their parents' voices quite happily and some added such comments as:

"Mummy's voice is all high when she says 'Get up' in the morning."

"Soft," said one; another: "Kind."

This is a way of starting aural memory development.

It is also important to draw attention to the importance of

silence. Just as we can learn to appreciate the spaces between shapes in a drawing or painting, so we should learn to appreciate silence, and the children should be made aware of it. To encourage this awareness we introduced some games to a class of 35 six-year-olds, who entered enthusiastically into the fun.

The children were told to lie down, with eyes closed, and to listen to any sound made by their bodies.

Richard's voice piped up: "I can hear my heart beating."

Mary: "I can hear a kind of *mmmm* sound," (a soft high *m*).

Teacher: "Can you make a soft sound?"

A soft breathing sound was made.

Teacher: "Just keep your body floppy and relaxed. Now choose a soft sound to make with your tongue."

Soft tongue-breathing sounds emerged.

Teacher: "That's good. Now, look up at the space above you. Make your sound a little bit louder. Throw it all into the space above you." *m m d d eem eem.*

"Choose a harder, louder sound to throw into the space above you."

Various loud *rrrm* and *errm ermm* sounds filled the hall.

Teacher: "Those sound like a lot of motor car engines. Can you choose a hard sound and throw that into a space? Then listen to the silence when you stop."

The children absorbed their silence.

Teacher: "Think of your name, just think it, don't say it. If there is a hard sound in your name, make that sound just by itself—throw that sound into a space."

ggg, ccc, pp, and other sounds came from the floor.

Teacher: "Make a sound and then have a silence while you think about your sound."

Child: *naa*—(silence) *naa*—(silence) *naa*—(silence).

Teacher: "Do it again, so it's sound and a rest, sound and a rest. Start when you are ready."

Children: *naa*—(rest) *naa*—(rest) *naa*—(rest) *naa*—(rest).

An interesting point about this is that each child was working independently, ignoring the sounds and silences of those around him and carrying out his own pattern of sound and silence. The fact that they were lying flat and throwing their sounds up into the air helped their feeling of isolation. Various sounds were made, and though some children achieved a hard sound, more were content to make it loud.

Teacher: "Close your eyes. Jeremy, please do your hard sound for us."

J ———— J ————— J ————— J —————

Teacher: "Try it once more with a longer rest, so that everyone can listen to your silences or 'rests'."

J —————— J —————— J ——————

Teacher: "This time all try to have a long silence or rest."

ss —————— ss —————— ss ——————
err —————— rrr —————— rr ——————
k —————— k —————— k ——————
d —————— d —————— d ——————

Teacher: "Now try to change the pattern by making your sound and a quick silence—a short 'rest'. Mark, try yours."

m m m m m m m m m m

Teacher: "How could Mark make it different from just, *m m m*?"

Lizzie made a *mmm* sound which came in short bursts, each *mmm* starting low and moving to a higher note. The notation to explain them was written by the children.

Lizzie:

Teacher: "What is she making it do?"
Richard: "Go up and down."
Teacher: "Was she? Lizzie, do it once more."
Richard corrected himself, "Making it go up."
Teacher: "Now, all of you, think about your sound, and then do your sound and silence or rest; make the sound go up and down or stretch it."
Children: (a sharply defined sound).

Teacher: "Make a pattern with the ups and downs, but don't forget the silences."

18

Children: (a flowing sound).

Teacher: "Listen to John."

John:

Richard: "That makes a sort of tune."
Teacher: "Choose a few different sounds with a rest."
Child: *pppppp ppp p p pp*
Teacher: "Listen to one which is a lot of short and long sounds drawn out. Richard, just do yours."

Although the children involved had been trained in aural discrimination and perception since their school entry, this was the first time they had been asked to use their voices specifically in this way. The children's attention had not before been directed to and focused on the making of such sounds and how they could be altered or elaborated. The added enjoyment and concentration were not the only results. The children's awareness of the use of "the rest" in traditional musical notation and practical work was deepened. Some were made more aware of the role of silence in music making, as they had used a rest in a way they had not consciously realised before. Because the approach was fresh both to the children and the teacher, perhaps a greater degree of concentration was achieved, as they were

19

using their knowledge of a musical principle in a new way.

Another benefit arises from the use of a technique new to the children and perhaps new to the teacher. Because there will be no previous experience of the ideas about to be used, there can be less danger of a "teacher-imposed barrier" appearing. The teacher cannot so easily say unthinkingly, "Oh, young children couldn't do that; anyway there would be chaos, Johnny would just scream and be silly." Often we need to try something completely new to make us realise that children can often cope with and produce more than they are sometimes allowed to do. When listening to the tape after the session, the teacher can also often pinpoint her own mistakes. Work which trains teachers and children to become more selective in their listening habits is very valuable. A teacher's expectation can make the most significant difference to a child's learning.

One day, a class of 34 five-year-old children went into the playground and described the sounds they had heard.

Birds squeaking
Lorries going *mmm m m*
Someone slamming a door
Footsteps and someone talking
Mrs. Mansell's bike, *click, click*
Sparrows on the roof, *chip chip pe pe pe pe chip chip*
The wind rustling through the trees, *ps ps ps ps*
Children talking.

The following are some of the sounds which the children thought would be heard in the summer:—

Lawn mower *br br br kkk bbbbb*
Aeroplane in the sky *eaweaweaw*
Jet overhead *pppkkk*
Daddy mending the car *kkkkkk*
Baby crying *aahahah uhuhuh*
A fly *ssSSSSsss*
Pulling grass with your hand so it squeaks—*kee kee kee*
Cars—nasally *eeeeee*
Throwing stones on the ground *boink, boink, clop, tic, tic, tic.*
Electric saw cutting trees *zs zs zs zs zs*
Wasps *bsbs bsbs*

Some children are like sensitive microphones in that they can hear everything that goes on, but they are not selective in their listening. To encourage aural discrimination we played some games.

We took the children outside and said: "Sit as quietly as you can and listen for three soft sounds."

Here are some of them:

A piece of paper flapping against the waste paper basket.
A visitor's dog panting.
A rabbit chewing some lettuce.

Back in the classroom we asked the children to sort out some of the sounds we had heard. We discovered sets of low sounds:

A Hoover
A lawn mower
The kitchen potato peeler

and high sounds:

Birds *chip chip*
Bee *bzee bzee*
Squeak of grass pulled through their fingers.

There were some lower "high" sounds:

Girls' voices
Ladies talking softly
Small dog barking

and higher low sounds:

Men whistling
Big dog barking
Boys talking

There were loud sounds that were long:

A helicopter flying low
Bus going by
Lorry

and these had sounds which were short:

Car horn
Man hitting metal
Kitchen Supervisor chopping mint

They heard long quiet sounds:

A fly
The wind in the trees
Hum of a potato peeling machine in kitchen from distance

·and short quiet sounds:

Violins playing pizzicato
Footsteps in the playground
Bouncing rubber ball

It was clear that not only did the children listen carefully and try to analyse the sounds that were made, but they were also using their aural memory to draw on those sounds they might hear in the summer, thus helping the development of their memories.

Focussing attention on their quality, they became more aware of the sounds around them, often ignored as just part of a background noise.

Later we introduced some visual reinforcement. We asked the children to draw what the sounds out of doors would look like to them. Here are some examples.

1. Richard

An aeroplane getting louder and louder.

2. Edward

Bee.

3. Stephen

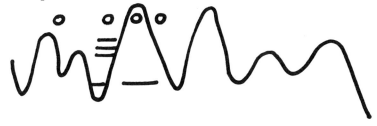

Sparrow cheeping and car going past.

Here two sounds were selected. The child was aware that the level of sounds varied and he represented the revolutions of the engine in the up and down nature of his drawing.

4. Nicola

Dog Woof

Musical Sounds

A dog barking while music was played.

Some children had given traditional descriptions of sounds such as "woof woof", "quack quack" and "cheep cheep", but, when they were encouraged to listen more carefully and to try to make up their own sounds, the woodpecker's "tap tap tap" became *tttt dddd ttt dddd* (spoken rapidly); and the wind through the trees became *ph ph ph ph*. (The teacher was interested to see that the child wrote down this sound as "ph" and not "f".)

Writing down sounds using what they thought were appropriate symbols became exciting for the children. This incidental phonic work was being done with a great sense of fun, and there were lively discussions when they were deciding whether the sounds were long or short, what symbols they should use and what words described their experiences. The exchange of ideas at this level began to enrich their vocabulary and stimulated those children who were not usually forthcoming in their conversation or ideas.

Examination of the characteristics of sounds, the exploration of relationships between them and discovering what they know about their own voices are the simple beginnings of musical thought.

Stories with sound

When we told a traditional fairy story of *The Three Bears* to some four- and five-year-olds, we experimented with instruments. The children decided that whenever Father Bear was mentioned a drum would be played; Mother Bear was represented by a tambourine, and a triangle was Baby Bear's own sound. In order that all the children were involved, other sound effects, made with their voices, were introduced, e.g. birds singing, wind rustling through the trees. This idea was carried over to their own stories.

Some older children from 5 + to 6 years old developed some "sound" story writing where they dictated their ideas to the teacher to write down.

A tree falls down *cr cr crack sh sh sh bang.*

The train goes along *ch ch ch ch chchch oooo teteletete letetete deded deddede.*

This is a calm sea *sswws sh sh sh* and an aeroplane is flying overhead *brm rm rm rm n n.*

The rough sea in a storm *ooo sh sh sh ch ch sho shooo.*

The little girl is playing in the wind *sshh ooooOooo shhshh.*

I like the noise of an aeroplane *mmmm aaaaa nnnnnn.*

The swing is squeaking *eea eea ee eaea.*

This kind of work was extended with some older children of 6 + who dictated or wrote their own stories. They suggested an accompaniment using more traditional instruments and made up a simple score which they could each understand and repeat:

This is Fiona's story:

Here is a house and a boy came out of it and he slammed the door and there was a ball that rolled over and hit the wall with a bang. The wind was howling and the smoke made a rustling noise coming out of the chimney and then there was silence. The wind had stopped, the door had shut, the smoke came out of the chimney quietly, now the ball stopped rolling.

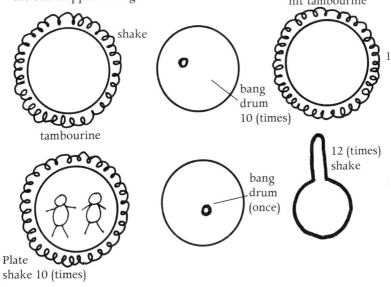

Another story went like this:

Here is a dog and he is barking. His best friend is a cat and they like playing ball on the short grass. The cat purrs and wags her tail and so does the dog.

Simple formal notation is taught by the teacher whenever the occasion arises. The children discuss walking rhythms:

and running rhythms:

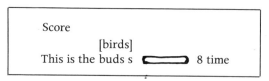

Then we clap them and compose simple rhythmic patterns. (See Chapter 3, pages 52, 63.)

One of the happiest outcomes of these experiments with sounds was the development of a boy, who, when he came to our school at the age of six, would hide away under the tables in the classroom and refuse to take part in school life at all. He would not speak to anyone and had no desire to read or write. After very patient treatment by his teacher he began to enjoy playing with bits of wood or sandpaper and anything that made a sound in the music corner in his classroom. He liked singing sounds and played happily on the instruments during the workshop sessions which occurred once or twice a week. He even wrote a story with a very simple score:

thee is to horses and 1 dog and sum seagulls and the seagulls are sigin and the horses are nain.

> Score
>   [birds]
> This is the buds s ⊂⊃ 8 time

(He shook the bells 8 times for the birds' song)

This was a tremendous effort for him to make.

Later he became quite confident in his actions, and when he left the school at the age of seven he could read quite well, was reasonably fluent in his conversation and had a great love of music.

Introduction of musical notation

Many teachers, in beginning the development of creative music, see it in isolation, and start with non-pitched percussion (instruments upon which one cannot play tunes, i.e. tambourine). This restricts the children's activities and no place is given to other sounds.

Teachers should not be deterred by the lack of expensive equipment. Junk material and voice and body sounds provide means of introducing basic musical principles. A group of six-year-old children arranged a varying-sized collection of beer tins and experimented with beaters such as sticks, spoons, small metal bars and the traditional beaters, to make sounds. They discovered that the larger tins made a deeper sound than the smaller tins, so these were then arranged in size and played again. They even discovered a simple chord of three notes, i.e. *doh me soh*.

Later the children composed a song about the tins. This led to a discussion of rhythms and size related to sound. Crotchets and quavers were mentioned only incidentally. We worked partly from a mathematical concept, dividing the notes by 2 then by 4 then 8.

The work did not depend on knowledge of formal musical notation, but, the teacher introduced it for the benefit of interested children. We found in our experiments in music that there is no rigid progression of work related to age for, as in all subjects, the rate of development depends on the child's ability, interest and natural talent. In the teaching of musical notation, some children carry on using their own form of expression when writing melodic patterns, tunes or sounds and then quickly progress from using, for example, *B A B A G* to formal notation. Others are more interested in non-melodic music, using percussion instruments (e.g. drums, cymbals, tambourines or junk materials] than in writing tunes. These children, nevertheless, also learn formal rhythm patterns.

The teacher discussed the conventional notation for the song about the tins and their music was scored in the traditional manner. The large tins were played as minims, the next size as crotchets, the smaller size as semi-quavers and the smallest were demi-semi-quavers.

French time names were used:

Taa-aa

Taa-taa

Ta-té

Tafatéfé

The beats were scored and a chart of coloured tins was made. After the rhythm had been established then the melody was added and the song which evolved went like this (C Major. Played on the piano by John and Elizabeth mainly using *soh* and *doh*):

Verse 1   Once upon a time there was a kitchen,
C   C C G C   C   C G C E

With tins sitting quietly on the shelf.
C   C   C G   C C C G   C

Red tins, yellow tins, green tins, blue tins
C   C   D D   D   E   E   F   F

Sitting there by themselves.
G G   G   G   G C

Verse 2   Suddenly an elf came to the kitchen
C   C C C C   C

Looking for something to do
C   C   C   C C

Saw all the tins sitting quietly by themselves
C C C C   C   C   C   C

And decided to create a hullabaloo,
C   C   C   C   C   C

Gave those tins some arms and legs
C   C C C   C C   C

Gave them rhythm too
C   C C G C

Made them jump down off their shelves
C   C   C   C C   C

Dance and skip like kangaroos.
C   C C C   G C

Dustbins went boom boom
  C   C   C   C

Coffee tins berroo berroo
  G   G   G   G

Spice tins clitter clatter, clitter clatter,
  C C   C   C   C   C

Small tins bitter bitter batter batter, bitter bitter
  G G G   G   G   G   G   G

batter batter,
  G   G

O what a jum, jum jerroo.
  C C C   C   C

Much freer work can be done with junk material than by always using percussion instruments. In fact, any material in the room, house, garden or playground can be used to form interesting groupings of sound which help to increase the sensitivity of the children to the sounds which surround them.

Every environment has a soundscape which can be explored by children to make music. Breathing, pencils on desks, fingertips moving on any surface;[1] metal rods, paint brushes on beer cans, dustbin lids and chain belts with variation in attack, duration and speed can all make interesting sound patterns.

One day, when tidying a class, David, a five-year-old, was carrying a small plastic chair across the room. He bumped the seat of it gently with his hand. Then, with great excitement, he turned to his teacher and said, "Listen, I've found a new sound; I can bump this," and he hit the chair seat with his hand, making a series of sounds. A few other children imitated him.

Then Peter said, "My sound is different!"

"Why?" asked the teacher.

"Because I'm moving my arms more quickly, and I'm making a faster rhythm."

Richard joined in, "I can join my sounds together." He started with the initial slow bumps, then increased the speed so that the sounds came more and more quickly, until they were almost continuous, and at the same time the sounds became louder. In these few minutes, the children had not only discovered a new sound, but had used it to reinforce their existing knowledge of two musical principles: that of accelerando—getting quicker—and crescendo—becoming louder. We always encourage them to use the correct musical terms. In this way the children absorb the basic vocabulary of music. It seems, from experience in this school, that very young children who have no pre-knowledge of conventional musical form and notation can quickly assimilate it and are able to appreciate the possibilities of sound patterns and equally quickly work out their own notation scores.

Peter, aged six, was playing a triangle and writing a score for himself. He had composed a rhythmic pattern which he set out:

Music for triangle:

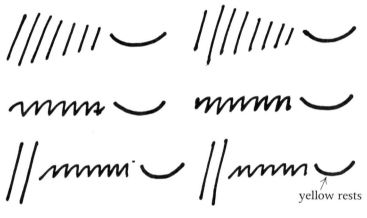

yellow rests

mark indicated
yellow rests

When the music teacher offered to play the pattern from his score she could not understand a yellow line which recurred at regular intervals.

"What is this meant to be, Peter?" she asked.

Somewhat condescendingly (as though it ought to be obvious to anyone!) Peter replied, "It's a rest of one beat!"

A class of five-year-olds experimenting with sounds from conventional instruments produced pictorial representations of sounds which were very easily understood and reproduced in sound by other children. We believe that sounds should come first in music rather than notation. This does not mean that one should not work towards conventional notation, but, if a child can repeat a sound pattern he has enjoyed by reading from his own score, we think this is much more valuable and exciting than losing his interest by imposing a more complex form upon him too soon.

Once a child has built up a vocabulary of sounds we have found that he will often look for a sound to fit a situation. For example, a class of six-year-olds making "machines" in movement brought in maracas, tins to be beaten, shakers and a drum and beater to augment the movements and increase the effectiveness of their dance. They also used their voices to make "machine sounds".

Use of the voice and body

The voice is one of the most versatile instruments which the children have, and small children used to shouting, screaming and squealing in the playground have little inhibition about the use of their voices. They will make high, low, sustained, quick, rough, smooth, happy or sad non-verbal sounds with their voices.

The music consultant had found it difficult to get very young children to use their voices to the full when they first came into school. Although she worked with the class teachers in their classrooms or in the hall, a method we call "co-operative" or "team teaching", she had always found these children a little shy when she approached them. One summer term she suggested that they sang some nursery rhymes. They waited for each other to begin and then sang very tentatively.

"Let's play a game," suggested the music teacher. "Choose a sound and, without screaming or shouting, let it come out of your mouth."

All kinds of high, medium and low sounds emerged, all very quietly.

"Now," said the teacher, "it doesn't matter if your sound isn't the same as anyone else's because it's your own special sound. Try again."

This time more sounds emerged and their volume and tone was very much improved.

"Now make a sound which you think is the highest you can sing. Are you ready? Think of your own special sound, open your mouth as wide as you can and sing it."

The children joined in with gusto. Already this singing game had given them the confidence to discover what their voices were capable of doing.

The teacher and the children discussed the expressions "high" and "low". These concepts are determined by our own voice and we had to try to put this over to the children in a simple way. We discussed the low notes on a violin, on a recorder, on a double bass, which one of the parents brought into school, and then the children explored their voices as we had explored the sounds on the instruments.

As their experience grew and they began to control their voices with any vowel sounds, the teacher asked them to sing some patterns of sound:

"Sing as high as you can."

"Sing as low as you can."

"Sing all the way up from low to high."

"Sing all the way down from high to low."

"In your own time, sing up and down."

It seemed there was no reason why children should not be able to sing as freely in the classroom as they do when they are skipping along the road or in the playground. Music should be a natural expression to them.

We encouraged the teachers to use their own voices and a tuning fork, if necessary, rather than the piano, in the initial stages of singing. So many songs have only a limited compass. It is fun to learn by imitating sounds.

We played at "echo" singing or clapping, when we asked the children to sing back or clap the echo to our sounds. A very easy one to start the game in the summer term, of course, was "cuck-oo", "cuckoo" or a child's name.

soh	*soh*	*soh*	*Da*
me	*me*	*me*	*vid*

Other consonants were incorporated and sung quickly or slowly.

dddd	*d d d*	*d d d*	*tttt*	*g g g*
fast	slower	slower still	fast	slower

Unvoiced consonants were used to vary a singing pattern.

ssss or *fff*—i.e. a sound where you don't actually get a singing
  tone.

dddd   *sssss*   *ttttfff*   *dddd*

The final result was very pleasing. Even the so-called "groan-ers", a name given to children who could not "sing in tune", were able to sing a note in their own range. Later on, as they gained more listening experience, we realised that most of these "groaners" were by no means tone deaf. We tried to sing with them at their pitch and so helped to extend their compass.

Response singing games, where the teacher sang a phrase and the children replied, were popular. They were sung like a question and answer:

        soh   soh
Teacher: "Robert"—   me   me

         soh
Child: "I'm coming"—   me
           doh

         soh   soh
Teacher: "Are you ready"—   me
             doh

      soh   soh
Child: "Yes I am"—   me

All these games helped to improve the children's diction and intonation during singing and also helped them to use their voices to full capacity.

Our bodies are basic musical instruments. It is easy to make

33

sounds by clicking fingers, clapping hands; hands tapping on shoulders, elbows, heads, knees, or any part of the body; hands rubbing quickly or slowly on clothing or on the skin of arms or legs; fists beating chests. Hands can vary sounds made by the voice, like the popping sound of a finger inside the cheek or whooping like Red Indians. All these activities can be used to create patterns of sound and scored in the children's own way.

One term a class of six- and seven-year-olds, whose theme was Time, were discussing Dinosaurs. They were fascinated by the sounds of such names as Triceratops, Stegosaurus and Brontosaurus, and they decided to make up a song about them.

Whilst some children were thinking about the words, others sang notes to make musical phrases. Each child in the latter group sang a different note until the phrase sounded satisfactory to them; then the words, which were being written down by the other children, were adapted to fit the tune. At this stage only their voices were used as instruments. During the experiment we discussed the kind of speech which would have been used by cave-men. Some thought that only vocal and body sounds would be used to communicate with each other, and so we made drawings of chants and body rhythms for the rest of the class to see and use. At this stage some children introduced a kettle drum, and the following picture shows their suggested body movements made to the names of the creatures.

"These are body sounds like the early cave-men made and patterns of sounds we made on instruments."

Igu ano
Igu ano

don

don

dinosaurs

dinosaurs

kettle drum

We used the drums a lot that went *berum*.

34

We then added body sounds such as beating fists or hands on chests and slapping legs, into the following song:

Dinosaur Song

Softly whispered: Dinosaurs! Dinosaurs! Dinosaurs!

Two Hundred Million Years Ago
In the Mezozoic Age, Ugh!
White hot matter fell from the sun
And became our big round world.

Body sounds to rhythm of song: Slapping body on chest with open hands or fists.

Dinosaurs were gigantic and fierce
And some had very sharp teeth.—Ugh!
Tyranosaurus was a tyrant king
Thundering and plundering went he. (Slapping thighs)

Slower, heavy arm movements. Beating clenched fists on opposite upper arms.

Brachiosaurus heavy and strong
Stayed in the water all day long
Munching plants so sleepy and slow
He could not fight, his legs would not go.

Quicker body sounds— Anywhere!

Ornitholestes, Oviraptor,
Iguanodon, Triceratops,
Stegosaurus, Brontosaurus

These are the names of the dinosaurs.

Softly.   Dinosaurs Dinosaurs Dinosaurs

Loudly.   Ugh!

Dinosaur Song

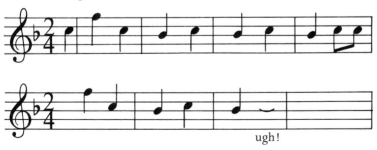

ugh!

35

While children are learning to control their sounds and we are encouraging them to become aware of their bodies as instruments, they begin to realise the qualities necessary to produce soft and loud, harsh and smooth, light or strong, sustained or short sounds. These experiences seem to improve their perception and handling of sound.

Controlling junk material

When the children brought their junk, some of the items such as the dustbin lid, nails, chain belt, and mugs, made a much better sound when hung up, but how could this be done? An old free-standing bookcase was not strong enough and it was liable to fall over. Then, leafing through an educational supplier's catalogue, we discovered a strong metal frame which was originally designed for the hanging of paintings or drawings.[2] We sent for this and found that as it had a good base with a firm frame it would suit our purpose.

Together with the children we hung the pieces of junk in various ways. Sometimes we hung them in sets, i.e.
1. All the pieces that made a high sound or a low sound.
2. In sound patterns chosen by the children.
3. Nails and plant pots were hung in order of pitch, i.e. high to low—from left to right as in most conventional instruments.

We were thus able to illustrate many basic musical principles quite simply, for example, that small objects make a high sound when hit and that the larger the object the lower the sound, as with such instruments as the violin, viola, 'cello, double bass etc.

There are also various lengths of pipe which make different sounds, i.e. short ones make high sounds, the longer ones low sounds.

When we had set up the frame we asked for suggestions for a name. Simon said,

"Let's call it a Set of Music!" Then after thinking for a moment he said, "No, we can't call it that!"

"Why not?"

"Because, when you make the sounds they change and so it can't be a set!"

We decided to call it a Sound Frame.

One day some six-year-old boys were experimenting with the junk material and were working out short sound patterns and scoring them. A very musical visitor was watching them and asked four of the boys to do the following:

1. Play their pattern.
2. Play it, then think it, then play it again.
3. Think it, then play it backwards.
4. Play it, then think it, then play it backwards.

The boys completed the assignment with flying colours, proving that their recently composed pattern was firmly fixed in their memories. As the children do not always have to score or write down what they have done, we were very pleased.

During one session three six-year-old boys played the open strings of the piano to make "space music" as a background for some dramatic activity.

"Are you going to score your music?" we asked.

"No," was the reply, "we'll be able to remember it."

Two days later we made two separate tape-recordings of their music on two separate occasions. The recordings proved to be identical.

Piano strings and vibrations

The old piano with the front removed has proved an invaluable source of interest and experience. With its help taped music evolved.

A class was asked to make storm sound effects as an accompaniment to their drama; a small group of children volunteered to try. We spent some time discussing the sounds leading up to and involved in a storm. First Robert, who had volunteered to be "the thunder", hit a bass drum very loudly.

Warwick, "That doesn't sound like thunder."

Teacher, "Why not?"

Warwick, "You should be able to hear it coming a long way off."

He fetched a wooden beater and hit the drum quietly at first and then louder.

Richard, "That's more like it, but it's still not rumbly enough. What about using the piano?" He depressed the loud pedal and played the lower register with his fist. "That's it!"

Warwick, "If we play the strings we'll get a louder sound." He found a wooden beater and played the lower strings from low to high.

Richard, "Yes—but we've got to make it come softly first and then loud and then go away like real thunder."

Warwick, "How can we make it go away softly? If I keep on playing the strings it just gets louder!"

Teacher, "One of you keep your foot on the 'loud' pedal and play one stroke across the strings and if you keep your foot down keeping the dampers off the strings—you remember we talked about this a few weeks ago when we were looking at the piano—the strings will go on playing for a long time getting gradually softer as they stop shaking."

Warwick—"Now we've got it!"

We then talked about lightning, how it was a sudden crack, and decided to play it on cymbals. For fierce lightning we added the sound of a piece of corrugated plastic strummed with a wooden beater. The way the storm progressed was determined by the drama. The children who made the music were conducted by Robert who increased the intensity of sound to fit in with the story. This tape played at half speed has been a most effective background accompaniment.

The Headmistress remembered that at one time she had prepared the strings of her grand piano with drawing pins to try to make it sound like a harpsichord. We thought we should let some children try a similar experiment with different articles. We tried rubbers which gave floppy, hushed sounds, and pencils which gave crackling sounds. Then we used plastic spoons and clothes pegs, making some unusual sounds which were reminiscent of oriental music.

Following these piano-string experiments and talking about them, the children became deeply interested in vibrations. We set to work to measure the duration of the sound and vibrations on different instruments, measuring with a stop-watch the length of time it took for the sound to die away. When we had timed

the duration of sounds the children suggested that we could put down the names of the children who played the instruments on a chart.

"Why do you want to do that?" the teacher asked.

"Because when Stephanie strikes the cymbal the sounds last longer than when Lynn does it."

This was very perceptive and we realised that the children had already grasped the principle that the duration of the sounds depended a great deal on the attack and force of each child. The chart showed the following results:—

	Cymbal	Triangle	Drum
Helen	3·6 secs	6 secs	2·5 secs
Amanda	3·8 secs	10 secs	1 sec
Nicholas	4 secs	9 secs	2 secs
Annabel		3 secs	10 secs
Jane		3·8 secs	6 secs
Stephen		3·5 secs	7 secs
Duncan		3·8 secs	10 secs
John	3·9 secs	4 secs	8 secs

John said, "It would be fun if we could see the vibrations on the drum like we can when we pluck the low string on the piano."

"How do you think we could do that?" asked the teacher.

"I know," answered Peter, "we could put something on the top of it."

"Something like . . ." started the teacher.

"Some unifix blocks," said Richard.

"No, they'd be too big." John broke in.

"Why?"

"I don't know."

"Well, find some unifix and we'll try," said the teacher.

They put some unifix blocks on the drum.

"They don't move very much," said John.

"But if we had something lighter," Richard burst in, "like cornflakes."

"But we haven't any cornflakes here."

"I'll bring some tomorrow," said Richard.

"There's some sand, can we try that?" asked Duncan.

"By all means!" They were fascinated by the movement of the grains of sand over the skin of the drum.

The next day they scattered rice on the tambourine and cornflakes on the drum and watched them move about the surface of the instruments as they vibrated.

The children were very excited to observe this visual representation of the vibrations. They vied with each other to make new experiments.

Mary struck a triangle strongly with the beater and when the sound had gone said that she could feel the vibrations through the triangle string.

The boys held some rubber bands between their teeth and twanged them with their fingers. They discovered that they could feel vibrations through their teeth, down their nose and along the cheek bones. Robert made a toy guitar by stretching rubber bands round a shoe-box, and the children quickly discovered that thinner rubber bands round the box made higher sounds than the thicker bands. They realised that long bands and short bands made different sounds, and adapted the lengths to make the required sequence of sounds. Then the question "Why" was asked.

We all decided to think about it!

When we experimented again with the long and short bands, we were able to explain that when a rubber band is stretched and plucked it moves backwards and forwards. This movement is vibration. You can also hear a sound. This sound is caused by the vibration. Sound energy is produced when something vibrates, and this sound energy can be heard. The faster the vibrations the higher the sound. The number of times an object vibrates is called the frequency. High frequency produces a high-pitched sound and low frequency a low sound.

An electric food mixer showed the children that as the speed of the beaters was increased so the pitch of the sound became higher. Then David held the mouth of a bottle to his lips and blew across it.

"I've made a sound like a fog horn," he said.

"Where does the sound come from?" asked Mary.

"It comes from the vibrating air in the bottle."

"What would happen if there was some water in the bottle?" asked the scientific member of the class.

John poured some water in the bottle and then blew across its mouth. This time the sound was higher and we concluded that it was because there was less air to vibrate. We then thought about some wind instruments and explained that a flute player blows across the sound hole of a flute in the same way as John had

blown across the mouth of the bottle to produce the sound.

This led to a discussion about our voices. We felt their vibration by gently feeling our larynxes as we talked. As we hummed we tried to feel the vibrations on our cheek bones or the tops of our heads.

"I think we've got our own musical instrument inside our throats," said Jane.

"That is what we call our voice box."

From there we went on to explain about our vocal chords and how the air from our lungs makes them vibrate. We said that when we speak or sing we stretch or loosen the chords to make higher or lower sounds. The children were deeply interested.

At another time we noticed that sounds vary in quality, i.e. the sound of a drum is different in quality from that of a violin. When violin lessons were taking place, we joined the class and observed how the vibrations combined to make this differing quality.

We borrowed an oscilloscope and watched the characteristics of sounds being reproduced as lines on the screen.

"What does the loud sound look like, Stephen?"

"Like waves moving up high and down low," he answered.

"What about the soft sound?"

"Well," Mary said, "a bit like the loud sound, but it doesn't move up quite so high or down so low as the loud sound.

Loud sounds caused the lines to spread further upwards over the face of the tube than the soft sounds.

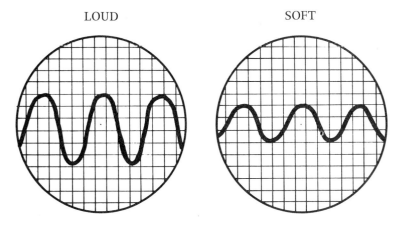

LOUD   SOFT

We discovered that high-pitched sounds appeared to have a smaller wavelength than the low-pitched sounds.

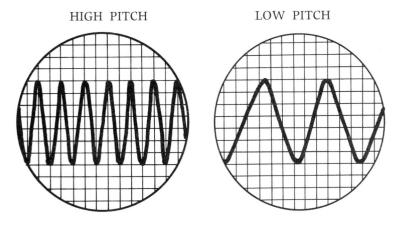

HIGH PITCH   LOW PITCH

The experiments with the oscilloscope tied in very well with the work on sound patterns which the children had composed themselves.

We talked about the use of sound in our everyday lives: as a warning, e.g. police cars, fire engines; as a way of showing happiness, e.g. laughing; to get rid of pent up energy or anger, e.g. shouting; as a way of making people happy, e.g. singing; comforting people, e.g. Mummy soothing a baby or child with words or singing a lullaby.

We went further and discovered from reading and talking to people about the use of sounds in man's work. Surgeons use sound in operations, sound vibrations are used to find weak places in metal, to mix paint and chemicals, to engrave on glass and to kill bacteria. We found out that fishermen use sound to locate fish.

"What about the sound barrier," said Michael, "can you tell us about that?"

"Let's look it up," we said. In a book called *What is Sound*, we read what it was and why it occurred.

These varying experiences help the children to build up their own encyclopaedia or memory bank of sounds. We are convinced that they should have the chance to experiment in these ways with sounds before starting to play an instrument such as the piano, violin or recorder.

As Kodály stated, "With a good musician the ear should always lead the way for those mobile fingers."[4]

References

1. John Paynter, *Hear and Now*, Universal Edition (London) Ltd., 1972, p. 27.
2. *E.S.A. 1973 "Vital Years"*. Cat. No. A7016/174, Storage Display Rack—on its own without any rack or storage baskets.
3. Reuben Collins, *What is Sound*.
4. Erzébet Szonyi, *Kodály's Principles in Practice*. Boosey and Hawkes, 1973, p. 16.

CHAPTER 3

The Score

As the children grew more accustomed to writing down and reading back their elementary scores, they were led to use more conventional notation and musical terms. At the same time their inventive powers become more sophisticated, so that the music they created was more advanced. They quickly absorbed new traditional songs, and they exercised greater discrimination in selecting from records and tapes the kind of music which they needed for use in assemblies, or other activities such as Drama, Art and Movement.

Writing down patterns of sound to remember

The children had already drawn the shapes of sounds on paper (Chap. 2, p. 23). These shapes enabled them to remember what they had heard and to reproduce the sounds. This was a form of simple score. They themselves discovered the need for writing down something to remind them of what they had done. It came about in this way.

Thirty children, between five and six years of age, sat down to think about the various sounds that could be made with the different parts of their bodies.

Kevin said he could tap the floor with his feet, so we all tapped the floor with our feet. The tapping went faster and faster and louder and louder. Then Charlotte suggested we clapped our hands, so we did. David was clever and could flick his fingers. He was not the only one who could manage this, so we decided that those who could flick their fingers would do so, those round Charlotte would clap their hands, whilst Kevin's group tapped the floor with their feet.

When all the children were ready John signalled with his hand for them to make their different sounds. They all started together and the noise was a distinctly uncontrolled one; so we had to discuss how we could control the sounds and make them more interesting. Christopher suggested that we should start softly with the fingers flicking, then have a rest and have some feet tapping slowly and softly on the floor. Charlotte thought that we could make a loud clapping sound which went quicker and louder then slower and quieter. We decided to watch John carefully and when he pointed to our particular group we could make our sound.

Eventually this worked quite well, making perhaps a "sort of music", but it didn't sound quite right because sometimes it went on and on and was "untidy at the ends". The music teacher suggested that perhaps other sounds could be introduced to make it more interesting. Some children made breathing sounds like *h h h h* and added a few consonants such as *pppp tttt gggg*. Kevin said, "Couldn't *you* tell us when to make our sounds?"

"Yes certainly," said the music teacher. "Watch me very carefully and I will raise my hand when I want you to make your sounds. When I move both my hands apart, make your sounds gradually louder, and when I bring my hands close together, make a soft sound."

This we described as being like a conductor who helps an orchestra to make sounds and keeps them together when they are playing. It was very effective and some control came to the children's patterns of sound. She introduced silences or rests in between the sounds and the children responded well. When John was asked if he could conduct the group like that, he said he could not remember how it went.

The only answer to this was to make a score so that he could remember what to do. The teacher asked for suitable symbols. After a great deal of argument and discussion we came up with the following:

Clapping   slow   faster   very fast

Flicks ✓ ✓ ✓ ✓ ✓ ✓ ✓ ✓

Foot tapping o o   o o   OO
              soft   loud   louder

Breathing h h h h h h h h h

These results were interesting, as all the children drew bigger symbols for louder noises and showed the duration of time by putting down the marks close together for rapid clapping and farther apart for slower clapping. This seemed a good time to tell the children about the correct musical expressions for soft and loud, i.e.

pp—pianissimo—very soft
p—piano   —soft
f—forte   —loud
ff—fortissimo —very loud

They liked the sound the Italian words made, and practised them with great enthusiasm: so we incorporated the correct musical expressions, but the children did not wish to put in the formal rest sign because they found this too complicated at this stage and one boy used a yellow line. This was the final result:

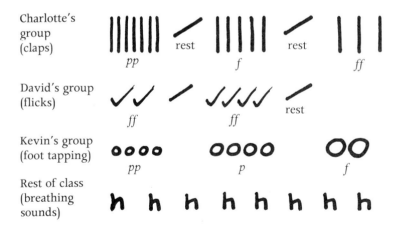

Charlotte's group (claps)
|||||| / rest ||||| / rest | | |
pp   f   ff

David's group (flicks)
✓✓ / ✓✓✓✓ / rest
ff   ff

Kevin's group (foot tapping)
o o o o   o o o o   O O
pp   p   f

Rest of class (breathing sounds)
h h h h h h h h

During the next workshop session the children wanted to make some more sounds of their own. John could not think of a

53

new sound until he heard a piece of kitchen paper slip to the floor.

"That makes a sort of slippy sound," he said. Charlotte's eyes lit up as they looked at a pile of newspapers in the painting area.

"Let's do something with them," she said. So each one of us took a piece of paper and sat down on the mat. Then they flapped it, waved it and shook it with gusto. When everybody was quiet again we asked several children to demonstrate their own particular sound. One discovery was that the *Daily Telegraph* made a different sound from that of the *Daily Mirror*, owing, of course, to the size and quality of the paper! They then chose the sound they would like to make and joined a group making that sound.

The groups went on experimenting, and we asked them to describe in words the sounds they were making with their paper, i.e.

Flicking
Tearing
Patting—palms of hands on paper in the air
Patting—palms of hands on paper on the floor
Waving paper
Tapping with fingers on paper held in the air
Tapping with fingers on paper on the ground
John suggested that they could make a paper orchestra.

We discussed how this would be done. Finally they chose the paper they liked the best and, with 4–7 children in a group, arranged themselves as follows:

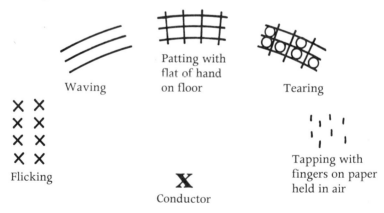

Waving

Patting with
flat of hand
on floor

Tearing

× ×
× ×
× ×
× ×
Flicking

X
Conductor

Tapping with
fingers on paper
held in air

The teacher reminded them of what movements she would make for loud and quiet sounds. Then she stood where all the children could see her easily, re-emphasised that they must watch her carefully, especially when she pointed to different groups and when there were silences or rests.

They began. The children had remarkable control over their paper and the sounds were unusual and pleasant. Afterwards some children offered to conduct and were quite successful in their attempts.

During a further session, Ian suggested that they could write a story or a poem and make some sounds to go with it. This proved to be very popular and they experimented with different types of paper, such as tissue paper or cardboard sheets. Some of their paper sounds were recorded on tape to see what they made us think about:

Waving cardboard	—Like a storm coming
Waving newspaper	—Rushing wind
Crumpling	—Like a fire
Tapping softly	—Like rain

Other five-year-olds had been experimenting with some traditional instruments that they liked, looking at their shape and the sounds they made. Finally they each took a tambourine and discovered many different ways of playing it. One flicked the skin with his fingers, another tapped the wooden side of the ring, while a third child scratched the surface of his tambourine. They had a heated discussion on the correct way to hold the instrument. Eventually one remembered that they had been told to put the index finger through the hole rather than the thumb, because it could be hurt.

Finally they asked the teacher if they could play their tambourines to the rest of the class. Each one showed a different method of playing it. Four of the children wrote the following scores for their performance:

SCORE FOR TAMBOURINE

Hitting (6)

Symbol chosen by:

Alexander

||||||

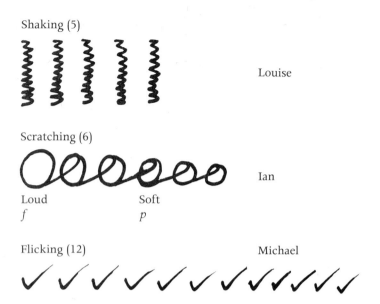

Shaking (5)

Louise

Scratching (6)

Ian

Loud
f

Soft
p

Flicking (12)

Michael

Afterwards other children suggested different ways of playing a tambourine. Bob decided that it made a harder sound if hit with the back of his hand. Andrew discovered that by rubbing it on his trousers it made a nice soft sound.

"It's funny," Mary laughed. "If I lick my thumb I can make it jump on the top of the skin." Then the teacher explained that if you lick your fingers and thumb and run it round on the skin this was called a finger trill. She showed them how to hold the tambourine slightly at an angle when it was being played and agreed that the instrument should be held with the index finger through the hole. Much incidental teaching of such techniques can be given during these sessions.

In another classroom, two children were exploring the process of composition, starting from the work on some sound patterns they had made. Mark had often worked in the music area and had got together an extensive collection of sounds. Its junk material ranged from pieces of corrugated cardboard, tissue paper, silver foil, the last two pinned on a wall, a cross-section of a log to a home-made chordal dulcimer, and a shaker made with different lengths of old wooden rulers joined together with string at one end.

John, through his friendship with Mark, had begun to work more freely in the music area and was creating his own patterns of sounds in a more confident way. One day Mark evolved a very rhythmic pattern, using his voice and the enamel bowl as a drum. At the same time John was making louder and louder sounds (crescendo) on the chordal dulcimer. He plucked the strings at random and then with his whole hand swept up and down the strings, varying the pace. As Mark's voice grew louder, it interrupted John who stopped to look at him. Watching this, the teacher suggested that, when they had worked out their own sounds, they could both try to work together; "Listen to each other's sounds, see what they are like, and you may want to join them up somehow. See which of yours, Mark, sound the best to go with some of John's sounds."

The boys listened to each other and then made their sounds together. John stopped and said "That's no good—it just goes on—it's not proper sounds." The teacher felt pleased that they had noticed the difference between random noise and an organised sound.

"We'll start quietly, like I did with my voice," Mark said, "and get louder, and then quiet again, so it's . . ." and as he searched for words, he moved his arm through the air, going up and down once. He began hitting the upturned enamel bowl with a metal spatula, making a short, short, long, long, short, short, long rhythm, then pointed at John who immediately elaborated on this with the chordal dulcimer, plucking three short notes, then striking the strings with the flat of his hand. Mark ordered "Now louder" and John swept the strings up and down trying to get a louder sound and making a "glissando". Mark hit the enamel bowl with his hands, in two groups of four beats, ending with one loud strike, and then his voice took over, with three *ooo-oohs*, each one ending on a high loud note. John tried for a really loud sound with his voice, making an *ooooo-ooh-ooh-oh-ooooo*, a kind of Red Indian war-cry sound. Mark echoed this, ending with four separate *oohs* but more quietly. He then hit the bowl again, let a silence occur, and repeated this. As he did this, John quietly plucked the individual strings of the chordal dulcimer at random, both of them instinctively getting quieter, till the sounds died away. The two boys then painted the score as follows, so that they would not forget.

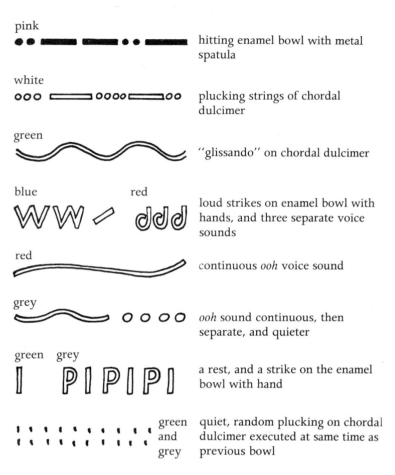

pink	hitting enamel bowl with metal spatula
white	plucking strings of chordal dulcimer
green	"glissando" on chordal dulcimer
blue **red**	loud strikes on enamel bowl with hands, and three separate voice sounds
red	continuous *ooh* voice sound
grey	*ooh* sound continuous, then separate, and quieter
green grey	a rest, and a strike on the enamel bowl with hand
green and grey	quiet, random plucking on chordal dulcimer executed at same time as previous bowl

When the teacher asked them how they had written down the sound pattern, it was obvious that some symbols had been chosen because their shape mirrored the movement of the sound they wanted. When Mark hit the enamel bowl four times, using each hand alternately, and repeated it, finishing with one strike, he painted this as WW ⟋. His voice making the rising sound of *ooo-ooh* was shown as ♪, the symbol showing the movement of the sound. In the score, the crescendo section was painted in bright blue and red, as the boys thought these were "loud" colours, while the quiet beginning and ending were painted in pink, grey and green.

Junk score and composing

One morning, when about ten children of 6 + were in the work-shop experimenting with junk materials, John picked up a piece of twisted wood shaving and commented that it reminded him of a cymbal going round and round. The rest of the group then began to search through the junk box for materials that reminded them of percussion instruments. A row of sticks were like drum beats, egg cartons the notes on a glockenspiel, and twirled white tape like Indian bells.

The children put these symbols on a nearby piece of frieze paper, about 5 feet × 3 feet in size. They seemed to equate "large" with loud, and so painted graduated rings round the drum symbols, the larger rings representing the loud sounds and the smaller rings showing the sounds dying away:

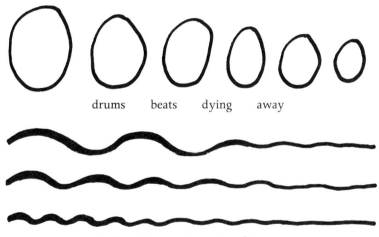

drums   beats   dying   away

Indian bell sounds getting fainter

This we called our "junk" score, and this first one was completely haphazard.

At a follow-up session the children were discussing a march by Sousa which they had heard during assembly. They were analysing in a very simple way the kind of music they had heard; why it made them feel cheerful, wanting to walk briskly or clap. They listened to the record again and decided that the strong

59

parts of the music made them put their feet down firmly when they walked. The teacher conducted by moving her right hand in time to the music, in a repeating pattern of 4 beats:

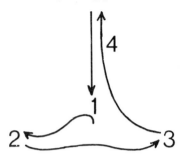

The children were delighted with this and asked about the people who played in an orchestra. They tried to identify different kinds of instruments and then returned to the conductor and the score.

In the end the children decided to compose a march themselves and eagerly chose suitable percussion instruments for their experiments. Having made their march to their own satisfaction, they used the junk materials to show the sounds.

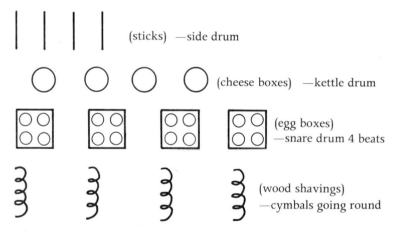

We were impressed by their great concentration on the quality of sound each instrument gave. This quality could be described in more sophisticated terms as "tone colour" or "timbre", and they searched very carefully for suitable materials to depict it. They also fixed a time for the march, counting 1, 2, 3, 4 across the score.

"Let's do it again," said Mary.

"All right," said the teacher, and she pointed out that in traditional musical notation the special repeat sign is :‖ . The children accepted this and incorporated it into their score.

It finally appeared like this:

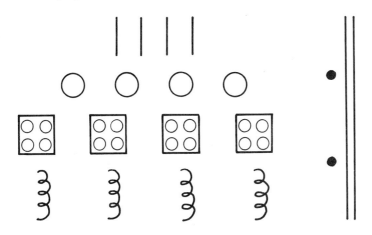

So, in a very simple fashion, they had composed a march, using the junk symbols to show them when to play their instruments. They were able to translate their score into sounds and thus make sure they could always play their march in the same way.

At this stage we were not concerned with the traditional notation of crochets or quavers and neither teacher nor children referred either to them or the tune. We were concerned only with the quality of the sounds and the children's visual interpretation of them, making sure that they understood the symbols which they had invented.

In this way the children were, in fact, discovering for themselves, by trying out different materials, something to express the sounds they made. This is the order in which a composer works. He usually thinks of his sounds first and then writes them down. The children were pleased to have learnt something of the meaning of the word "composed".

At a later date these children were listening to various march tunes in the school collection of records. They were discussing whether the march time was fast as in the Sousa March or slow and solemn as in *The March of the Hebrew Slaves*. The children discovered that whether the music was slow or fast they could still conduct the same four beats.

"It's like a trick," said Robert, "they've put lots of different notes in." He was waving his arms about excitedly trying to find the right words. "I don't mean the time," he added, "I mean lots of notes."

This seemed a good moment to explain how one beat might be divided up into so many notes. The music adviser suggested that they could collect words accompanied by their notation. The children offered words with one beat, such as "sand", "sea", "boat" and "house".

The teacher wrote them down with accompanying notation like this:

Other words were brought in and they were put down with their notation:

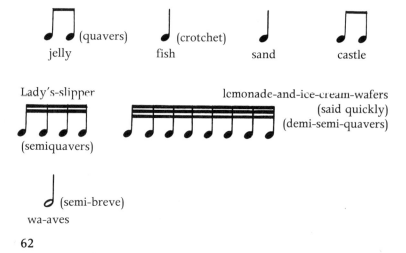

The children clapped the beat or pulse of the words and then made a rhythmic sequence of some of the words which was written down like this:

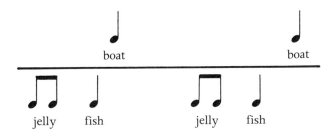

That kind of rhythmic sequence may be made as complicated as the children wish, and, in this instance, some instruments such as tambourines and chime bars were used to introduce added sound.

When the children first began to compose and write down tunes they did it in three ways. They composed a tune

(a)   for its own sake, because the children liked the sounds they made;

(b)   to accompany words which they had written themselves or to fit a poem from a book;

(c)   to fit a theme, e.g. the sea, space, or for assembly or dance-drama.

At first the music teacher restricted the children to three notes on the piano or to three chime bars of their own choosing. They played around with these notes until they had a recognisable tune, usually in an A B A shape, ending with a doh when possible.

Once Jeremy chose three chime bars, A B and C, and having played his tune he became quite agitated and asked for a G chime bar so that his tune could "go home". Instinctively he felt that the tune was in G Major and was unhappy until he could complete it. When he had played the tune two or three times to ensure that he really could remember it, the teacher wrote it out in the conventional way. This began *Our Book of Tunes*, which was proudly hung in the class-room.

Soon the children were no longer content with three notes or three chime bars, and when Richard wished to use the glocken-spiel to compose a tune he was allowed to do so. He produced a

63

very good little tune and wrote down this:

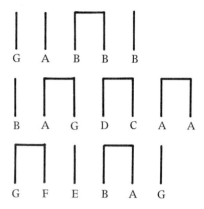

From that time on the teacher allowed the children to write down their tunes in any way they liked—as long as they could play them!

Most children used the letters already marked on the glockenspiel and xylophone, and they were encouraged to sing their tunes before they wrote them down. They wrote the phrases almost as they wrote sentences and then played their completed score. To help them with their writing we talked about notes which were "walking", i.e. crotchets, and "running", i.e. quavers. We brought in the French time names for these, Taa-Ta-té . We clapped rhythms and incorporated them into their little scores. When their rhythms became more complicated they went to the music teacher to help them write them down.

She also encouraged them to use the pleasing melodies which can evolve from using the Pentatonic Scale, that is a five-note scale. The notes CDFGA or CDEGA, DBF AB or GABDE were left on some of the xylophones or glockenspiels for the children to use. They generally found these notes easy to sing.

When left to themselves, with no guidance in the use of conventional rhythms of $\frac{2}{4}$, $\frac{3}{4}$, and $\frac{4}{4}$, some of their individual tunes had very unusual and complicated rhythms which even the music teacher found rather difficult to write down! The key centres also changed rapidly, as it does in some modern music.

Realising this, the music teacher introduced the music of such composers as Schönberg, Berio and Stockhausen's Electronic Music, *Song of the Youths.*

Composing to fit a theme

The children wrote music and songs to fit any theme or occasion. Once an admission class in their first term wrote a poem on "Taste" when preparing an assembly for the school. They made up a very simple tune clapping out the rhythm of the words, and developed a melody to fit it. Then these very young children volunteered to play it on the classroom glockenspiel, while the poem was gradually built up into a song:

Taste Song

G major

I like the food which my mummy makes

Thank you God for giving us taste

Fish and chips and nice little cakes

Thank you God for giving us taste.

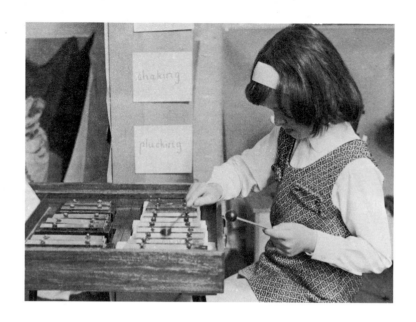

One group of five- and six-year-olds wrote a Christmas song for which Caroline sang a tune. She picked out the notes on a xylophone and wrote the note-names under the words.

(G Major)
Hurrah, Hurrah it's Christmas Eve
B   D   C   B G   B   A   G
We'll hang up our stockings tonight,
D   E   F♯   G A   B   A   G
And if we get a lot of gifts
B   D C B G B A   G
We'll jump and we'll skip with delight
    D   E   F♯   G   A   B   A   G

(D Major)
Let's listen, Let's listen,
A   A A   A A A
We're hoping to hear
G   F♯   F♯ G   A
Father Christmas slithering down the chimney
F♯   G   A A   A   B   C♯ D′ D′   D

(G Major)
Hurrah, Hurrah it's Christmas Eve
B   D   C⋅ B G   B   A   G
We're so full of joy tonight.
D   E F♯ G AB A   G

The *Dinosaur Song* (Chap. 2, p. 35) was the first class song composed primarily by using the voice. We wrote the first line of the poem:

Two hundred million years ago

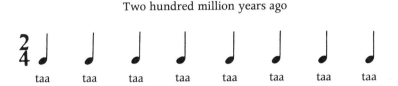

taa   taa   taa   taa   taa   taa   taa   taa

Having clapped the rhythm, the music teacher asked for a volunteer to sing a tune for it. Louise sang out boldly. We then found her notes on the xylophone and wrote them down. The next line is

In the   Mezozoic   Age

ta té   taa   taa   taa   taa   taa-aa

This time Caroline sang a tune and we wrote down the names of her notes also. This went on until the first verse was finished. We then wrote the words on a big chart with the note-names and the rhythm underneath each word. We found it was not always the same children who sang out their tunes, for on this occasion a very shy girl gave a significant contribution to the song and she was very proud to have it incorporated.

Occasionally the children reject a phrase or one child may subtly alter another child's phrase to bring it into line with the rest, but, so far, this has been happily accepted by the children concerned. We discussed the time, found the "heavy" beats and marked in the bar lines accordingly.

67

This was the final score for the tune:

Dinosaur Song

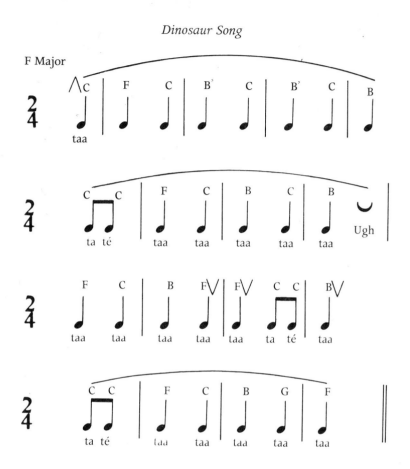

Sometimes we found that the tunes inside a child's head are much more sophisticated than one would expect. The *Colour Song*, written by Sara, Fiona and Gregory, children of 6 +, was a case in point. They each chose to sing their tune to the words. It was very difficult for them to sing because of the unusual intervals but the tune fitted the mood of the words.

> Red is happy, gay and bright
> Running full of joy.

Blue is a bright colour
Not always
Sometimes it is gloomy
dull, nearly grey, and then it is sad.
The sky is blue,
Also the sea.
When it is sunny the blue
is light and gay
When it is stormy, it is dull and heavy
Do you like blue?
I do.

Grey is lonely
Dull as a stone
But a rabbit is
frisky and happy, though
his fur is grey and white.

These tunes were not written down, but recorded on a cassette tape-recorder.

During the last week of the summer term we mislaid a hymn book, and the teacher whose class was taking assembly was upset because the hymn fitted her theme so well. As she had a copy of the words one of her class said that they could write their own tune. We clapped out the rhythm of the words, and then asked for some ideas for the tune. This time the children found the notes on their recorders. It was interesting to notice that the words were not contemporary and the class composed a tune which could only have been a hymn tune, finishing on a plagal cadence, that is to say ending as most conventional hymn tunes do with Amen.

We have noted that whilst children would put movement to sounds or sounds to movement with ease, so far, they had put a tune to words, but not words to a tune. Some children soon tire of just writing down the names of the notes for their tunes and need to progress further. These children are helped to think where the bar lines should be put by finding the "heavy" beat of the tune. When they have discussed this with the music teacher they write in the time signature.

We showed those who asked how to write the treble clef, and we introduced them to the easier key signatures of G Major,

, F sharp, and F Major , B flat, which they had come across in recorder, violin and piano lessons. We taught them how to read the treble staff, which they think is much easier than learning to read! We played games with flash cards, showing for example:

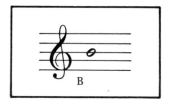

The children guess what the notes are or play "snap" with a selection of cards, one showing the name of the note and another the note on the line or in the correct space between the lines.

We taught the names of the lines, sometimes using the mnemonic Every Good Boy Deserves Fruit:

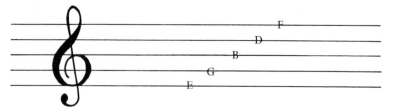

and the names of the spaces, i.e. FACE

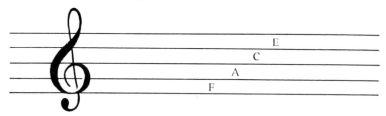

We showed them the notes on the piano, glockenspiel and xylophone so that the children could understand their relationship to the notes on the staff.

It is most important for the children to have had plenty of experience with sounds and rhythm before putting down the signs on paper. But when they wished to write their own tunes in traditional notation they had already had considerable experience of clapping and tapping, walking and skipping rhythms.

We used more sol-fa games (Chap. 2, p. 33) to train the ear to be aware of the intervals between the notes. We sang *doh* and then asked the children to sing *soh*—

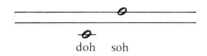

doh   soh

Then we asked if anyone could sing *me* followed by high *doh*, or when the teacher sang a high *doh* they were asked to sing a low *doh*. We did not make the games too complicated because it is quite difficult for children to pitch *fah* (4th) or *lah* (6th). (This will be discussed further in the next chapter.)

When we introduced these games at first we used only those lines of the staff which were necessary for our purpose. Some children wrote their tunes in this way, but we realised that other children wanted their music to look like "real music" and when they sang their tunes or composed them on the recorder they wanted them to look like other recorder tunes in their books.

When any children reached this stage, which was usually towards the end of their period in this school, we gave them some music manuscript paper for their work. At the same time we valued just as much the work of the child who came to us clutching his piece of paper on which was a line of marks and letters which helped him to hear and understand his own personal music which might have been written at home.

We have all met the music student who can, by counting lines and spaces and learning some rules, produce music written according to the rules of harmony, but cannot, until she reaches

the piano, actually hear what she has been writing. Our children are, we feel, nearer a true appreciation because the sound is first within them and however they write it down, the sound is the music and is all important.

We hope that we have shown that we do not dismiss traditional notation. We teach and encourage it side by side with the less traditional approach which we have evolved.

CHAPTER 4

Singing for Fun

All-round musical development of young children should include class or group singing and most children love to sing. But sometimes there are difficulties. Babies have their own singing language when they croon away to themselves; toddlers make up songs and skip along as they sing; and then, all too often, young children come to school where a formal "Singing Lesson" is inflicted upon them once a week round the piano. They are first taught the words by rote, sometimes with no interest or enthusiasm for their meaning, and by the time they have learnt them and music has been added line by line, all idea of singing and enjoyment may have gone. A class of eager young five-year-olds lose interest in singing very quickly when they have been told for the third time "Now, let's go over the words again."

Overcoming vocal difficulties

As already stated, we have found that very young children have been shy of singing when first coming into school. They often arrive at school these days with little experience of nursery rhymes or simple songs which used to be sung by their mothers, and it is necessary to remedy this. Singing songs to pre-school children is, in our opinion, as important to the development of their love of music as reading stories to them is to their reading development. Our group of 15 newly admitted children made hardly any sound when they were asked to sing a song, even after several days in school; this had to be remedied so that the children could realise their own capabilities. After first working with sounds we began with a so-called singing lesson described in Chap. 2, pp. 31–32, when the teacher asked the children to think of different sounds, which they sang in their own rhythm.

There are many possible variations in these early approaches. The teacher could have asked for long sounds:

aaah   *oooo*   *eeee*

which may be sung as high or as low as the children wished, or quick sounds:

pppp   √√√√   *bbbb*

which they could sing as quickly as possible to a note they liked.

When they had practised these, they then made up their own simple singing patterns. The teacher should always stress the quality of tone by encouraging them to sing "as beautifully" as they can or to "try to make a lovely round sound". She must emphasise the use of the tongue and teeth for the consonants, of a round sound for vowels—good articulation should be encouraged from the start—and, above all they should try to make as pleasing a sound as possible.

As these exercises are carried out, the children will become aware of the strength and possibilities of their voices without having to worry about words, tune or time-keeping. They will also become aware of the need for breath control. Some little children try to sing when breathing in. Jane, aged five years, always sang her songs breathing the words in with her breath. After practising sound patterns she realised that when she breathed in her sound disappeared for a short time!

It is important to have a well-ventilated room and to encourage the children to sit up or stand up straight, in a relaxed position but not stiffly. In fact we have often asked a class of 30 children to "loosen up" before a lesson by pretending to be floppy rag dolls. To help them to feel what it is like to breathe properly we have let them lie full length on the floor where shoulders are not easily moveable, and they then breathe from the diaphragm as they should.

For a change the teacher sometimes incorporated conventional musical terms into their sound patterns. She drew a pattern on a large sheet of cardboard and asked 10 children to sing the pattern to *ee aa oo*

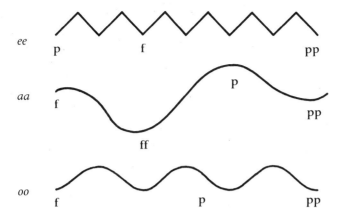

This particular pattern involved vowel sounds, but other patterns could have incorporated consonants or even words. They could be as complicated as the teacher and children wished.

Such games with patterns help children to control their breathing and sing pleasantly in tune. Some find this easier to do than others, but we do not know why. Many factors must be involved, and we find it difficult to say without further research whether this is a stage in their development or whether they have inherent physical difficulties of hearing or control over their vocal chords. However, some of these children eventually sing in tune if they are sung to and encouraged to sing on their own. Yet a few children, however much encouraged, still find this difficult when they leave the school.

Some children can be helped by getting them to whisper, speak and tap word patterns which include names of familiar objects and people. When playing "echo" games (Chap. 2, p. 32), we let the stronger and more able singers stand near to the children who were having some difficulty; they were encouraged to listen to their neighbours as they sang. But we never stopped or in any way inhibited a less able child in his singing because of his performance.

When it came to teaching songs we have observed that if the teacher chooses a song wisely, one that is within the children's range, about nine notes above middle C, with a good rhythm, and one that they enjoy singing, then they will learn it quickly. A teacher once told the story of a new song so that it caught their interest. She then sang the *whole* song. (Children are not hyper-critical of the quality of the singing and many infant teachers could sing to the children, even if they do not consider that they have a "good voice"). Having then asked the children to join in whenever they could, she sang the whole song over again a number of times. Whenever they found a difficult part they repeated it until they knew it. It should be stressed that it is not necessary to go on too long with a new song. It is better to move on to some well-known song before the children tire.

Specific vocal work is best unaccompanied, if possible, so that the children can hear themselves clearly. They need to know what it feels like to produce good tone, and become interested in the sounds they were singing. One class of six- to seven-year-olds felt their cheekbones, larynxes and the tops of their heads. This led to a discussion on sinuses, the spongy bones which make up the cheekbones and which help in the resonances. Humming is one of the best vocal exercises and the children enjoyed this. Listening to their own voices on tape is another way to train and develop sound discrimination.

Easy two-part singing

We have also played musical games, using the voice to develop an appreciation of time. Small children, as a rule, do not think in the conventional times of $\frac{3}{4}$, $\frac{4}{4}$, $\frac{6}{8}$. They generally use their own time scale to express their own compositions. So we decided to start a group of 12 children of 7 + to 8 years on a simple score on which we aimed to fix a time scale and relate it to their singing. In this way teachers who have had little experience in music could begin to develop a new approach to singing in which knowledge of traditional music is not absolutely necessary, and where the results could form a good base for later work on singing-games and songs of definite rhythm.

The teacher drew a line from end to end of the blackboard and told the children to choose any note they could sing comfortably to *aah* and to sing it as she drew her finger along it.

She then drew her finger from left to right across the line on the blackboard. The duration of the sound, that is to say the time scale, was controlled by the movement of the teacher's finger along the line. She moved her finger as slowly or swiftly as she wished, and the children learned to control their sound and to stop immediately her finger stopped moving. In fact, the teacher fixed the time scale and the children related their voices to it.

1. _____

   aah — — — — — — — — — — — — — — —

The teacher then drew two lines of different length with a space between.

2. _____ rest _____

   aah — — — — —   *aah* — — — — — — —

Again they chose a note and sang it while the teacher drew her finger across the line, with a rest between the two lines. The class was divided into A and B; one half sang the top line whilst the rest sang the second line. These two exercises were then sung together and the result was very simple two-part singing.

1. _____

   aah — — — — — — — — — — — — — — —

2. _____ rest _____

   aah — — — — —   *aah* — — — — — — —

There was no conscious counting of time as the duration was indicated by the teacher. These games help the co-ordination of the eye travelling along the line together with singing a sound. This developed both hearing and sight in a left to right movement.

Since children can count regularly the next stage was to fix a more definite time scale of 1–10. The teacher asked children to think the numbers and sing their sound as before:

1. _____

   1   2   3   4   5   6   7   8   9   10

Then the time scale was broken up.

2. _____   _____

   1   2   3   4   5   6   7   8   9   10

The children were again asked to think the numbers as their eyes travelled along and to stop singing at 5 where the line was broken. The teacher conducted this.

The children now sang these two forms again as a two-part song with the repeat sign at the end, the parts being interchangeable between the groups.

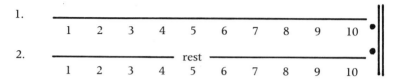

To obtain a more interesting pattern some of the sounds were loud and some soft, and here we used the conventional music terms of **p** soft, **pp** very soft, **f** loud and **ff** very loud. When written the music looked something like this.

1	2	3	4	5	6	7	8	9	10
p			p		f				f

We then looked at the quality of the sounds and introduced the signs meaning

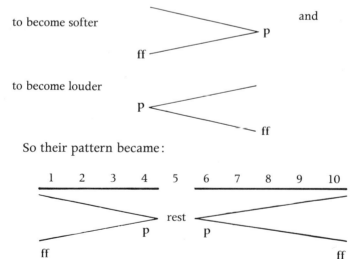

to become softer   and

to become louder

So their pattern became:

78

Later the teacher varied the sound and silences.

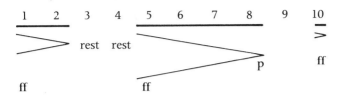

and a simple two-part sound pattern was:

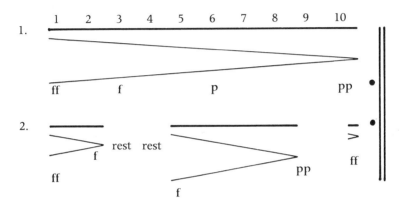

This simple introduction to two-part singing helped the children when they came to the rather more complicated two-part songs written in the traditional manner. The children soon enjoy singing rounds such as *London's Burning* and *Frère Jacques* if they are tackled in a simple way. These are a good introduction to two-part singing and the children exhibited a great sense of achievement when the rounds were accomplished. We do not think that in teaching two-part singing the teacher should tell the children to put their fingers in their ears and listen only to their own voices. We consider that to learn to sing a two-part song, it is necessary to listen to the other part and harmonise with it.

The work we did on the simple time-scale scores, where the children hold a note of their own, helped them to hold their note against another note.

When the children had fully understood what they were doing, the teacher changed the time scale and made a more complicated score which helped them to practise phonics, using the sounds *m g t*.

She asked the children to see if they and their friends could find a pattern of quiet and loud sounds of their own. In these later stages of sound development the visual reinforcement was important because it helped to develop a crispness and accuracy in consonant sounds and an understanding of musical terms.

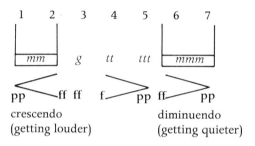

To develop sound and voice control we used another kind of score which helped to discriminate between "high" and "low" and at the same time developed the children's vocabulary of vowel sounds. The children chose a note and sang *a* as in "cart" and changed to a lower sound and sang *o* as in "boat" without sliding from one to another:

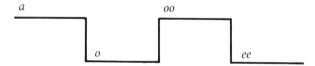

Sometimes the teacher gave the children a note to see if they could sing this pattern clearly, all together, the quality of the sound being very important.

A local musical festival

A week before the local music festival we thought that we could perhaps sing something different from the usual traditional songs.

The music teacher asked a group of about 25 third-year children from 7–8 who had been "brought up" on our principles of music teaching for a phrase which could be broken up into vowel and consonant sounds. They suggested SKY LAB. After much experimenting a sound pattern evolved as the children suggested how the words and sounds should be arranged.

The teacher wrote down the score, and the children prepared to sing it. Each child chose his own notes within the range of sounds where he sang most happily and comfortably. They then divided themselves into groups of high, middle and low sounds.

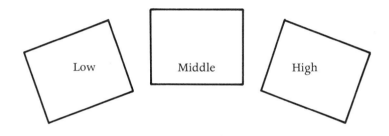

Some of the so-called "growlers", mostly boys, came in the low contingent, and used their often considerable vocal power to advantage. They sang freely and with enjoyment because they were not made conscious of any difference in their voices except that they were nice and low, and indeed were able to sing "high and low" in their chosen range, so they felt that they had some control over their voices. This gave them confidence in their singing.

The teacher conducted the group to guide them within the bounds of sound and silence, soft and loud, quick and slow and so keep some shape to the soundscape.

We were surprised, as we constantly are, by the quality of sound and by the understanding of the children as to what was required. After a few practices we realised that the sound seemed the same each time, even though the children had

81

received no guidance as to what note to sing beyond high, middle or low. We could only conclude that they had learnt the sound sequence they were making as they rehearsed. This is the score which the children wrote on a large sheet of paper.

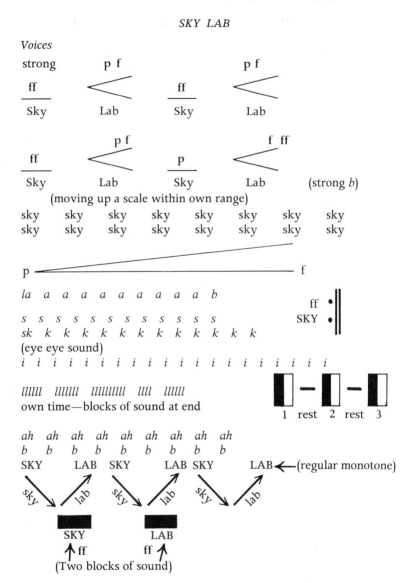

SKY LAB

Voices

82

There was an interesting reaction when this score was shown to a class of younger children of between 6 and 7. They sang it spontaneously!

As a result of their experience in part singing and harmonising with each other, the "sky-lab" group of children asked if they could sing a descant to a song called *Summer*. Caroline, who had a particularly clear, sweet voice, together with five other children, developed a simple tune with the teacher which was a third above the rest of the children. The result was very pleasant to hear.

As already stated, there is no reason why sol-fa should not be introduced at an early age in a very simple way. We have played games in which we have called out the names of children such as:

F Major

soh doh   doh soh
Mary   Sally

or sung the name of each child with a suitable tune and rhythm. This corresponded to the natural speech pulse of the names and obviously varied with each name. The children enjoyed these games and we found it a good way to memorise rhythms and intervals.

C Major

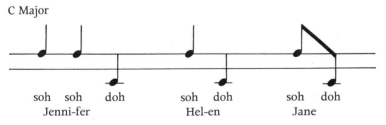

soh soh doh   soh doh   soh doh
Jenni-fer   Hel-en   Jane

We made a chart of each child's name rhythm and tune in sol-fa.

We found this experience helpful when we came to talk about the rhythm of songs and it was a valuable aid to aural training when we collected rhythms of the same kind in different songs.

Sometimes, in teaching simple sol-fa, the teacher's hand can be used to represent the five-line staff. The children in the 7 + age group have readily sung music at first sight where there has been the sol-fa notation.

Although a growing number of song collections are being published, there appears to be a lack of song repertoire for children in the 6–7 year-old age group. This does not inhibit us because our children have always been ready to compose their own songs and we have found many English folk-songs such as *Ten in a Bed, Old Macdonald had a Farm* and *One Man Went to Mow*, which the children have enjoyed singing.

We are convinced that singing to the children should be within most teachers' capabilities. We are fortunate in that the teachers in this school do not hesitate to sing folk songs and almost anything that they enjoy singing whenever possible. The children thoroughly enjoy this and ask for more!

We think that a music lesson should be planned so that some principles of music are involved but that there should always be room for the children's creativity and interest to direct the lesson. The good teacher will know where to intervene to guide their work into traditional channels or to explore the possibilities of the sounds we make today, for, as such *avant-garde* composers as Schönberg, George Self, and Cornelius Cardew have shown, the soundscapes used by today's and tomorrow's composers will not be fitted into a five-line staff.

CHAPTER 5

Music, Movement and other creative Arts

We realise the need for children to have many different experiences and tasks, and we encourage them to talk, so that they meet words in differing situations and begin to understand their many meanings. We want them to enjoy music, poetry, prose, drama and movement, and have discovered that music has stimulated their imagination in all these activities.

Music in all its forms seems inseparable from movement and we use music in the development of movement and movement in the development of music. Dancing and physical activity are stimulated by accompanying vocal sound and instrumental music, and the children's musical activities often call for corresponding movements to fulfil the creative urge within them.

For some children the outlet for the creative urge is in writing, drawing, painting, collage, clay and movement. We have found that music stimulates the work in these areas. We have found, too, that the effect of music on all these arts has been reciprocal. In other words, language, movement and art have helped to develop music and music has had a similar effect on these activities. It has become increasingly difficult to separate the creative arts, for each has become dependent on the others in such work as drama, assemblies and music festivals.

Many children react naturally to most musical experiences by painting or drawing quite spontaneously. They wish to picture the sounds they have made or heard. Here are some impressions given by five-year-olds:

Judith painted a picture and even wrote a sentence in it.

85

This is
a man
playing
some music

Michael's interpretation of a glissando on a glockenspiel was something like this:

Graham drew the sounds of Christopher's cymbal on a stand.

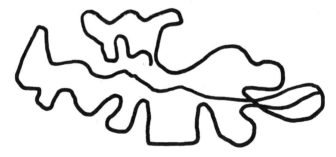

When Richard, aged 6, had listened to a record of Saint-Saëns' *Carnival of the Animals* he produced a collage to illustrate the *Royal March of the Lion* using some of his mother's precious bits of fur for a mane. He insisted on putting round it some drawings of the music :—

The whole picture was entitled :
The lion and its music from the Carnival of Animals.
He then wrote :

The lion roars like a brown thunderstorm and he walks softly He pads quietly He pounces stiffly He holds his red meat and bites it all round and tears bits off

Shapes in movement

Another class of about the same age was doing some work on geometrical and irregular twisted shapes. The children attempted to make geometrical shapes in movement, i.e. "tall", "thin", "round" and "star shapes", and these were represented in tissue paper, sticky coloured paper and collage. Later, after discussions and movement on irregular shapes—in particular, twisted and contorted shapes, accompanied by the tambour, triangle or wooden blocks—these children painted vivid and exciting pictures of themselves moving, with patterns of their movements.

Another group of children who were between 5 + and 6 + thought about the importance of shape in movement and the

87

teacher found an opportunity for a simple scientific debate on the pictures which they brought to illustrate their meaning.

The aeroplanes are not like they used to be now they are more like an arrow and they are able to fly through the sky quickly without the wind being able to push it backwards

One boy brought two pictures, one of a mini-car and another of a fast saloon car. He wrote:

Here is a car it has a big body and it is high it is like a square box but the other car is much flatter like a long rectangle The little one is bigger but I think it will go faster because of its shape and it is lower.

The group of children wrote about their ideas on shapes and chose a suitable musical background for their readings. This project is more fully developed later in the chapter.

An essential development in the young children who are exploring new realms of experience is the ability to express their ideas in words, and we have found music can be a vehicle for this. Its link with the other creative arts has added to the children's interests and enabled them to write down for others how they feel.

Dawn:

I like music because it makes me happy I like pop music and church music

Nicola S—:

I like music because I like Playing the tambourine.

Nicola T—:

I like to sing and dance to music and I like to play music and I like to make music up and play the music I makd up.

There should be every opportunity for flexibility in the work which is done in the classroom.

For one term Shapes was a class theme. As time went on the children became more aware of the shape of everyday things around them, and began to collect unusually shaped objects. They discovered that polystyrene tiles and odd pieces of polystyrene were an excellent medium for shaping pictures and models.

In Drama the children made individual shapes with their bodies: "small", "large", "smooth", "round", "tall", "spiky" and "peculiar". At first they all stood to make their shapes, but gradually some changed to using varied positions on the floor.

Later they worked in pairs, and then in groups. They began to talk among themselves about the kinds of shape they could make. These activities were sometimes accompanied by a drum or a tambourine. The teacher encouraged the children to describe their actions, and some drew pictures of their experiences and wrote under them:

> These boys are making a round and a spikey shape. Look at their spikey fingers. Look at the round shape it is a long one.
> The children are making shapes. One is a curly shape and one is a spikey shape made by two children. The curvy shape is made by one child.

Other children went outside to look at some smoke from a neighbouring chimney, watching the patterns it made as it curled upwards, sideways and downwards, changing direction very quickly with the wind. The shapes seemed to make something like the letters o, x, c, i and z. After watching these shapes the children pretended to be the smoke and their body movements showed how the wind changed the smoke.

At one stage they decided to make a "shape machine" with their bodies. The children made machine noises and each chose to dance a part of a machine, e.g. cog, piston, wheel. Then they moved into groups of three or four and danced around each other, each pretending to be a part of a machine. They made their sounds to accompany their dance, and, later, in the classroom, they decided to interpret their movements by making a frieze.

The children worked out the layout of the machine on a rough diagram and then discussed with what junk they should assemble the machine. This was laid out on the frieze so that plenty of

89

re-adjustments could be made. The children painted the material, glued the pieces on and erected the frieze in the classroom. It was about six feet long by three feet wide.

After a day or two someone suggested that the machine was too silent, and must come alive. After much discussion the children decided that it should make shapes.

"I know," said Robert, "what about putting a lump of wood in the machine? Then as it goes through it could be stretched, squeezed, bumped, spun and hammered and then it comes out in strange shapes!"

They worked out different sounds for the various sections of the machine, and decided to write them down so that they could be remembered. They then put the sounds by the appropriate bit of the machinery and pinned the result on to the frieze.

Sometimes the whole class became the machine and worked together as parts of the machine, incorporating drums, cymbals, bells and junk materials. At other times groups were formed to follow one after the other when the frieze machine was "switched on".

Here is the sequence of the sounds:

The machine in operation—*cr, cr, cr* (churning wood slowly); *sh, sh, sh* (quickly going up the pipe); *pk, pk, pk* (dropping slowly into a machine); *brm, brm, brm* (the machine whirrs round); *eeeee* (shooting it up another pipe); *O O O o o o* (down) and *de, de, de* (the prongs get to work—smashing, bashing); *boom bang* (shot out like gun fire at regular intervals into the container); *buzz* (swishing and swirling round); clonk (shapes are taking "shape"). They twirl up the last polystyrene pipe. *Plop* —the shape is released from the machine!

Shirley, a little girl who had great difficulty in reading or writing because of an unusual defect which caused very restricted vision in both eyes, used to be unsure of herself, frequently crying and complaining of sickness. One day during a movement session a teacher observed that, although she was a heavily built child, she was moving carefully, sensitively and with a firmness of balance. Sometimes she made quiet movements followed by stronger movements; sometimes her heavy movements changed to floating movements with a rare sensitivity. Her teacher praised her. Shirley's happiness and confidence grew from her love of movement. Her reading improved, largely, no doubt because of her teacher's help and the acquisition of new spectacles, but she also approached her work more confidently and no longer looked so worried. She mixed more freely with her peers. One day she painted a picture full of movement in blocks of blue, black, turquoise and yellow touched with red and green. She described her picture to her teacher.

> The boat goes *swish swash*,
> *swish swash*,
> The sun shines down on the water
> The waves are big and small
> *Swish sh sh sh*

Activities involving shape, movement and music sharpen the children's perception. When a group of children made movements with instruments or just with their bodies they became more aware of the meaning of such words as "sharp", "spiky", "round", "quiet", "loud", and were able to write with more understanding.

Jonathan described a kite flying:

> What I like about kite flying
> Is the heave on the kite string.
> Thin but strong
> The whistle of the wind
> As it rushes past
> Then swoops and dives.
> It rushes past again
> It stays up—then
> The wind completely dies
> The kite is fallen into a bush
> I untangle it unharmed,
> And put it away
> To fly another day.

Claire's feeling on riding a bicycle:

Swishing, cycling down the hill
Turning round corners smelling the fresh air in your face
In bridges out bridges up the hill so slow
The trees rustling in your ears as you go.

Robert S— made a realistic model of a horse and rider which gave the impression of movement and wrote these words:

Galloping hooves
Swaying tail.
Neck stretching
I feel like a bird in the air.

We believe that the permanence of learning is based on understanding and discovery, when the children do not work necessarily at the same pace but when, in their enthusiasm, they can talk to other children or to an interested teacher about what they are doing. This approach earns respect for what the child has to say or offer. The children in this school are free to develop their own particular interest in their own time, although we do not condone idle play and aimless experiment. The work must be purposeful. We try to help children to assess, observe, summarise, understand and think out the results of any work in which they are involved. (Chap. 3, p. 57).

One day a class of 6 + to 7 + were moving to "pop" music. Their teacher invited them to watch each other or to think about the kind of movements they were making to the music. This led to some stimulating conversation between them. As a result a few children decided to make some of their shapes in string. The theme for the term in that class was Colour, and it happened that one boy had found some brown raffia to represent his movement.

He told one of his friends:

I've made a brown shape. It reminds me of a brown crab and it reminds me of a brown cuberd as well. I made a bendy shape.

This spurred on the others to use colours.

Sally's lively picture had this sentence beneath it:

This is me and I am going mad and my hair is all running down my face: My dance is the colour purple.

James described his partner outlined in orange string:

Claire thought very carefully about her shape:

My shape is a cartwheel. I did it with my body and my hands. When I did it I had to spring right over so that my legs went up in the air I think blue is a happy colour to go with my happy shape.

93

Michael's was different:

i have done a picture of a string shape and the picture is red because it is a strong shape. We danced to pop music and it was lively like a party

Records and movement

Later in the year this class made a study of wild animals—the way they lived and moved, the noises they made, and how they killed their prey. After watching animals moving at the zoo the children simulated their movements. They used such descriptive words as "slithering", "hissing", "sliding", "lumbering", "loping" and "graceful" for snakes, giraffes, elephants and peacocks. They used Saint-Saëns' *Carnival of the Animals* again as a background record to play to their movements.

Under a magnificent crocodile made from egg-boxes and rough canvas Robert wrote this:

If I was a crocodile

I am a crocodile.
Mostly I like being in the mud.
I walk slowly. I can eat people.
Some men can shoot me.
I go in the water. I like it in
the water.
I like going deep down in the water.
I swim at the bottom of the creepy swamp
I can fight with my tail. I can waggle my tail too.
On the top of me I have got sort of spiky knobs that can

stick in my enemy. I eat all kinds of creatures that I kill.
I like to be a crocodile because I get good dinners
I crawl through the jungle, heavily
slow sloppy through the jungle.
The jungle shakes.

Each week a record was chosen by a teacher or child and used as "The Record for the Week". This was played as the children came into the hall for assembly, and the teacher in charge usually told them all about the record: which country the composer was born in and when he died; the time of the music, e.g. $\frac{4}{4}$ if it were a march, $\frac{3}{4}$ if a waltz. We discussed whether the music sounded English or Spanish or Russian, and thought of the general character of the music, e.g. happy, lively, sad, and what it made the children think of.

After one assembly a class of 6–8-year-old children were stirred by the march called *The Entry of the Comedians*. They asked to hear it again because it sounded like a circus.

Their teacher put on the record during the children's movement session and they tumbled about like clowns and performing animals; some pretended to be trapeze artists. The whole thing caught the imagination of the children. Ultimately they created a story about a ringmaster and a magician who released the animals from their unnatural bondage as performers. The children who had been moved to write about a circus read their story about the animals. Other children were performing animals and the whole scene was lively. The music on the record set the scene and the mass of tumbling performing clowns was controlled by Roy as the enthusiastic Barker who proclaimed "Roll up, roll up, come and see the animals. Roll up, roll up . . ."

Those children who had been to a circus wrote about their impressions. Diana wrote about the trapeze artists:

> The trapeze artists go springing up the ladder.
> Swooping and swinging about.
> They go spinning and spiralling round
> They are very acrobatic.
> They cling to each other
> very tightly by the wrists
> They hang suspended in the air.
> The audience is hushed.

The Fisherman's Song

Not all studies of this kind start from music as did *The Circus*, but in almost all of them music appears in some form. Another successful project was on Fishermen. The children made a large book illustrated by paintings about them. It started with the caption *A fisherman's life is a hard life*, and was followed by descriptive writing by about six children from 6+ to 7+.

Their interest in this theme led to their making up a *Fisherman's Song*, the words of which went like this:

> Heave, ho, away we go,
> Pull in the fishing net,
> Heave the winches,
> Heave ho, away we go.
> Open the cod end
> Take out the liver
> Heave ho, away we go
> Gut all the fishes
> Wash them clean.
> Powder them with powdered ice
> Keep them freezing
> Keep them freezing
> Throw out the net
> Till we get to the shore.
> Heave ho, away we go.

The tune was made up by the children with the co-operation of the class teacher and the music teacher. It developed into a two-part song. As the boys were singing they spontaneously made the movements of heaving on the ropes, pulling in the nets, cutting open the fish and gutting them. The girls decided that the wives wouldn't be in the ships, but would be left at home worrying about their husbands. They organised themselves into groups, some waving goodbye to the fishermen, others mingling amongst them carrying their imaginary baskets of fish, and singing,

> Fresh fish for sale
> Who'll buy my fish
> Fresh fish for sale.

The music teacher gave a definite lead to this "descant". She helped them to sort their ideas by giving them soh and doh in the chord of C Major.

Fish Descant

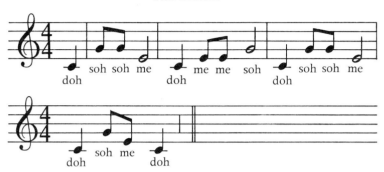

Fresh fish for sale

Who'll buy my fish?

Fresh fish for sale.

They found this "singing over the top" of the boys easy to do because of their previous experience of sol-fa.

This simple two-part song was very effective, and another group of children wanted to add instruments to give rhythm and harmony. They chose the xylophone, recorders, snare drum and maracas. Every child in the class contributed to the ultimate shape of this work. In the end we sang it for the local non-competitive music festival.

The County Adviser for Speech and Drama once asked a 35-strong class of children aged from six to eight to work out a presentation, lasting ten minutes only, for the drama festival. The scene was to be at sea in modern times, but the children were somehow to introduce both time past and time present.

After several ideas had been put forward, the children finally decided on a theme which they called *The Land that isn't there*. This involved sounds, movement and a story about strange creatures and a cloud which so influenced a modern ship that everything mechanical—radio, watches, engines—stopped.

After a grand fight with these creatures, the cloud disappeared and all went back to normal.

This production involved vocal sounds, and they used some sounds recorded from a synthesiser from the Music Workshop at La Sainte Union College of Education. This is an instrument made up of dials and controls using oscillators, filters and reverberators to produce "electronic" sounds.

There was great scope for the children to use movements such as slithering and sliding, gliding slowly and quickly. While they performed their actions they talked spontaneously. They enjoyed this, and it was all completed within a few days so that the children's interest, spontaneity and freshness were retained.

We discovered that the interaction between music, painting and other crafts, drama and movement occurred naturally, without any contrived situations. The motivation came readily from the children.

Developing movement

We used various stimuli to develop movement but we tried to ensure that these did not detract from the basic qualities of their movement training. Young children need to be aware of themselves, of their bodies, for instance by lying on the floor, sensing where the body is, and then standing up.

Movement concerns the whole child. It helps physical control and self discipline, encourages the development of the mind and spirit and the control and use of the emotions and breaking down self-consciousness.

When the children first came into school at 4 + and 5 years old, we practised walking, running, jumping, skipping and hopping. We encouraged them to explore their bodies, to look at their hands and watch them move, to see what they could do with their arms, legs and feet; to feel for example where their neck and head were.

We watched the children during their play times. Even some of the youngest and less confident of them eventually moved freely, exploring all the play areas and apparatus with energy and enthusiasm, flinging their arms out, spinning round, jumping and leaping over the playground markings—the widening brook, stepping stones and lines and circles.

This confirmed our ideas that almost all movement is purposeful, that a child naturally responds to and communicates through movement. We have often noticed that children will make movements to describe something for which they cannot find the words. One authority, who has made a study of slow readers, has said that he considered good motor activity to be the foundation on which a child's learning rests.

By constant practice we helped them to improve control over their bodies: to stop and start moving again; to use different parts of their bodies to lead their movements, e.g. following their arms, elbows, noses, chins and ears.

During one course which we attended Cecelia Lustig, who worked with Laban, the great exponent of movement, said that in her view, children were born with certain movement pattern characteristics and that we could help to develop their full personality. Those with quiet personalities could be helped to be strong; some who were direct perhaps lacked diplomatic qualities. Others who were sensitive and careful might lack firmness of balance in outlook.

The children became aware of the different qualities of movements as they responded to different timbres, for example, the sound of a drum as opposed to the sound of Indian bells. They built up a vocabulary of movements—e.g. heavy, light, quick, slow—just as they built up a vocabulary of words.[1]

We noticed that young children, watching the teacher as they moved, tended to concentrate on only one part of the body at a time. They had to be encouraged to watch themselves dance and to use the whole body, even when the arm or hand was leading. As they became more successful, their good bodily movements helped them to become more self-reliant and self-confident.

One of their difficulties, we noticed, was to make full use of the space around them. We spent much time on this aspect of movement, in determining whether they were using up a lot of or just a little space. "Look around you—feel the space behind you, in front of you, high above your head, on the floor." Children learnt at different rates. Some were confident in their movement from the beginning and would stretch and spring into the air or leap across the room with freedom and abandon whilst others developed strength and mobility more slowly.

One of the aims of movement training is to "quicken the senses and cause them to register experience more vividly",[2] and, in so doing, develop the child's flow of movement. One can see such a flow when a child has organised a series of instruments and is playing a tune, his arms, shoulders and body moving in a deliberate but easy movement. Controlled and efficient use of the body is essential in music as it is in movement and drama.

Each movement of the body is characterised not only by its shape, but by its duration. Realising this, a teacher asked a group of young children to explore a specific movement at one time. They concentrated on standing still in a space and, from this starting point, achieving a twisted position. At first, under her guidance, they thought of one body part at a time, starting with an arm, and twisting it, backwards or forwards, high or low. At this point some children needed to develop their awareness of joints! They then moved on to the torso, the other arm, legs and head, holding the position if they could. They tried to concentrate on the position of the whole body, relating each limb and each part of the body to it. This static experience, related to space and time, was quite different from a sustained float or glide movement.

Children whose twisted shapes were most capable of being held in a "statue" position were painted by others. The results varied from a painting of a person with squiggly limbs, to abstract, curled patterns, many of which revealed a good grasp of twisted shapes in relation to each other.

Some children saw only a dance pattern:

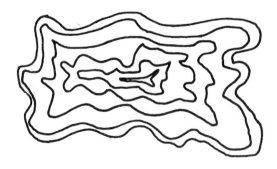

Others drew a figure and movements that the head, arms and legs made:

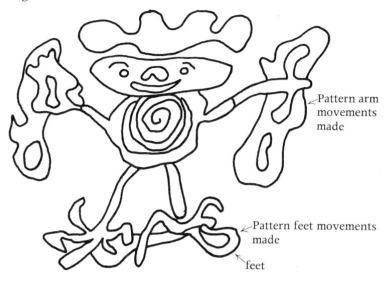

Pattern arm movements made

Pattern feet movements made

feet

Since some children were accustomed to making their own sound patterns and had explored various ways to start and finish, they applied this principle to their movement. When interpreting David's painting of a squiggly sound, made by the tongue revolving in the mouth   , the children had

only been concerned with the actual movement, beginning and finishing in a sloppy manner. Now many imaginative interpretations of the sound and its visual representation were tried out; John stood straight and turned backwards slowly round and round; Helen lay on the floor with her arms pointing above her head and rolled fast over and over; Jane did a cartwheel. Having evolved their individual interpretations, the teacher suggested that the movements needed a definite beginning. The children spent a few minutes in their starting positions in stillness and silence; when they were ready, they executed their movement, and finished quietly, holding their position. Younger children seemed to appreciate a definite beginning and ending more with a simple, single movement, which seemed to demand their attention for its own sake.

This group of children went on to interpret their personal sound scores in movement. They made the sounds themselves, wrote them down and then danced to their score. A child's score of

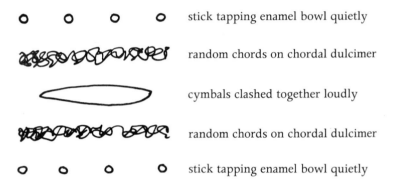

○ ○ ○ ○	stick tapping enamel bowl quietly
	random chords on chordal dulcimer
	cymbals clashed together loudly
	random chords on chordal dulcimer
○ ○ ○ ○	stick tapping enamel bowl quietly

was interpreted by starting in a low, curled up, crouching position. As each tap sounded, the child's clenched fist came out and struck the space on either side of his body. When the random chords were struck, he twirled around with arms and head flopping aimlessly, raising himself to a standing position, and jumped and clapped his hands in the air above his head with the cymbals. Then he twirled down to his crouching position flopping his head and arms again, where he repeated the three stabs with his fist, and curled up in his finishing position.

When we begin to think of movement in this way, both children and teacher will envisage many possibilities arising from various topics. On one occasion a piece of driftwood in the classroom led the teacher to see if the children could interpret it with a movement sequence. When asked what the shape made them think of, suggestions of "a gun", "a finger", "a bird with feathers", "a dog's nose" came tumbling out. When told to look at it more closely, a girl pointed to one end of the driftwood, where a sharp piece tapered, and, much to her teacher's delighted surprise, asserted, "That's like a quick . . ." and she flicked her hand up in the air to show what she meant.

When asked how they would feel, how they would move if they were that piece of wood, different children said, "smooth", "slow", "down there", pointing to the smooth section where the bark pattern started.

"And, having gone down, how do you get to the bit you call the 'quick flick'," the teacher asked. Looking at the driftwood again, several children called out, "Back up the same way, slowly, and then out and do a quick flick."

The children got into starting positions on the floor, some crouching and others sitting. They faced the teacher, watching her trace the movement flow of the driftwood, and all their movements were in a forward direction, more or less on the spot. Obviously they needed to relate to the flow of movement by watching the driftwood closely, concentrating hard on its changing levels. Later these movements were related to the musical sounds they worked out on their instruments.

Working with music scores as a stimulus, or with patterns in pebbles or driftwood, the children often create a sequence of movement. They need to discover the full range of movements their bodies can make, which parts can lead to a movement, and how the separate parts move in relation to each other and the body as a whole.

Sounds and movement

In our work with young children we have found that sound plays a dual role with movement as stimulus and accompaniment. Unity in sound and movement is shown by the sounds which come from the body itself. Hand clapping, or stamping feet emphasise the rhythm of the movement, and vocal sounds are particularly expressive, since they arise from the effort involved. Children should experiment and find out how body and vocal sounds can add to the quality of movement. Younger children may find at first that vocal sounds are more rewarding than playing an instrument and moving to it, as body sounds are part of the child's movement and dance. Indeed we have found that sometimes the use of too many instruments can inhibit the quality of a young child's movement.

We have used descriptive and action words to stimulate movement, where meaning, sound, or word associations have suggested the kind of movement to be performed. The phrase or verse thought suitable by child or teacher should be taped so that the children have a chance to listen to it two or three times. Readers will think of many suitable examples; among others, we used:

> Through Dangly Woods the aimless Doze
> A—dripping and a a—dripping goes . . .
> Slip-slopping through the bog and heather
> All in the wild and weepy weather.
>
> James Reeves.

Suddenly she spread her brown wings for flight, and soared into the air. She passed through the grove like a shadow and like a shadow she sailed across the garden.

Oscar Wilde.

> Slowly, silently, now the moon
> Walks the night in her silver shoon;
> This way, and that, she peers and sees
> Silver fruit upon silver trees.
>
> Walter de la Mare.

Pure vocal sounds have also been used. Children match movement with the flavour of sound in vowel sounds, consonants or syllables. It has not mattered if the sounds used were "nonsense" ones. *Ddddd* said in an emphatic way often results in a staccato, jerky movement, while *shooowoo shooowaa* would bring quite different results.

Music is chosen to set an atmosphere, or a mood as an accompaniment for movement. In some dramatic work based on the idea of landing on the moon, the children's movement was greatly helped by the taped sounds on a synthesizer. The tape had been made for a previous activity, but the sounds on it were more suitable than any other music they could find. It emphasized the quality of slow but sustained flexibility that the children were trying to achieve in their movements.

We use as many different ideas as possible to extend a child's movement and his awareness of movement to express himself. Interpreting the movement perceived in a pattern, a piece of driftwood or a flint, enlarges what we may call his "movement repertoire". With creative and imaginative movement will come the release and growth of the child's personality, making him capable of expressing his inmost thoughts.

Children find slow movement harder than fast movement. As many of them had watched "slow motion" on the television screen when a football player's movements had been shown, we suggested that they should try them out for themselves; this was most successful. Either as individuals or as group members they produce effective movements of throwing, stretching, pulling and pushing.

Afterwards Stephen wrote a poem:

Football

I like football
Running kicking!
Penalties are fun!
Scared, lonely
Nervous in goal
Tackling with force
Determination in your
mind, in your foot!
Hooray! We've won!

Words also were used to stimulate movement; the teacher suggested such words as "dab", "flick", "stamp", "thrust", "punch". She noticed that when the children made strong heavy movements they were also making involuntary sounds like "ugh" and "oogh". She seized on these sounds and, as an experiment, asked them to give her different sounds to which they could move.

The children soon understood the idea and gave various sounds, light ones: *pf, st, st, tp* and strong ones: *ning, eegh, aaargh* to which they moved expressively. One of them asked, "Can I do something and then see if the others can make some sounds while I am doing it?"

There were some interesting suggestions as to which sounds were the most suitable and the class split up into groups, each practising different movements with appropriate sounds. They did light, slow, heavy, soft, strong, leaping in the air, low-crouching down sounds and movements. Each group watched each other with fascination.

To develop the children's vocal range, the music teacher began very simply to link bodily movement with vocal sound. She suggested that the children choose a low note which they found easy to sing, to crouch down near the floor as they sang it and then let their voices rise to notes as high as they wished, accompanying this with movements at low or high level. They did this in their own time. The teacher explained that they were making their own personal music and that no one else could make sounds exactly like theirs or move in exactly the same way as they could.

The children became very absorbed in their sounds and movements. The youngest ones were able to join in and had no inhibitions when it came to making sounds and moving to them. After all, children do not always move quietly, but often make appropriate noises.

Dancing

Later on a class of children from 6 to 7 + began making patterns of sounds to accompany patterns of movement. Some chose swaying, soothing, lilting sounds together with appropriate movements; others chose to sing *dab, dab, dab* very quickly, moving their hands in and out of the space around them. Working in groups of four to five, each child chose his own kind of movement and appropriate sound, then wove them into a pattern.

Towards the end of the session they were asked to write down a pattern of what they had chosen to do and for this they chose coloured crayons or pastels. These are the results of some of the movements described:

1.   A swaying movement

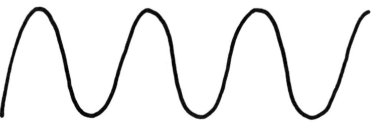

2. *Dab, dab, dab*

Nicola's pattern was this:

wsh wsh wsh went
this elliptical shape

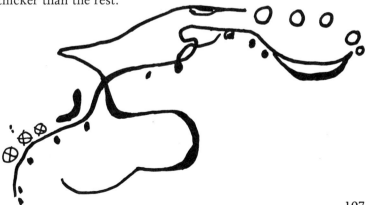

Spinning wheel
belt sound

Louise moved more positively. Her lines were broader and thicker than the rest.

Several of the class then came out at a time to dance their sequence, making their own vocal sounds to accompany their movements. One or two children had drawn a pattern involving more than one kind of movement and sound, and as time went on they became more conventional in their approach to dance and sounds, singing and dancing to sustained and staccato sounds.

Having danced as a class the children then split up into pairs, one child moving round the other with a high or low sustained or staccato movement according to the sound they made. They were told to watch and listen to their partner and then make their own sound and movement.

It is difficult to reproduce their sounds in writing, but this will give a rough idea of what the pairs did.

	ooooooooooooo	(rising and falling, drawn out, smooth high and low movement)
Pair A		
	bbbbbbbbbbbbbb	(short explosive sounds, quick running movements)
	eeeeeeeeeeeeee	(long, low sustained sound, low-level movement—smooth)
Pair B		
	w w w w w w w w	(high note, and dabbing movement at high level)

The teacher said that they could stop when they wanted, without waiting for everyone to do so. When they had all stopped and were resting, she began to talk about the quality of their movement.

"When we're making sounds," she said, "we must still make good movements to them, just as when we're playing an instrument. If you are making a lovely low sound, try to make a lovely movement to it. What would you do to Peter's long low sound?"

Louise said, "I'd try to go out as far as I can with my body or as far behind or to the side—"

"Yes, and use all that space," said Simon, "and put my voice into it as well."

"Splendid," said the teacher. "Now do you know what Peter's sound is called? It is a sustained sound. Do you know what that means?" Ian thought it sounded long and smooth. Flowing and soothing were other descriptions used.

"Do you know the name for those little short sounds you make, like *dddd* or *tttt*?" asked the teacher.

"Not really," said Ian, "but I think they're like the sounds we make on the violin, not with our bows but with our fingers—plucking the strings—and we call them 'pizzicato' then."

"That's a very good description," she replied. "When we play short notes in music we say they are 'staccato'. So yours could be . . ."

"Staccato sounds," called out Bobbie.

Later they painted their dance patterns. Jennifer painted one in black and yellow on a red and blue background.

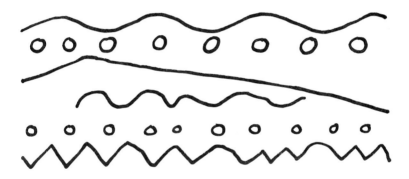

The children, having drawn a dance score, could both read and dance it. Their efforts gave an added dimension of sound, so that where the pattern showed a high curve the movement was high in the air and the voice was also relatively high. Some of the children went a step further and danced and sang their interpretation of another child's score.

The children much enjoyed this involvement of sound and movement, and some children, who, because of shyness, lack of interest or ability took little part in other activities, wholeheartedly joined in during musical activities. Dance can lead to a breakthrough in communication with the retarded child, satisfying his need for security and self-confidence. Michael, who

109

was such a boy, surprised them all when he volunteered to do his own dance and it came out well.

Young children are quite happy to concentrate on movement for movement's sake. On some occasions the movement brought forth a flow of language and on others the language produced movement.

Many other experiments were made in the movement sessions. One day the teacher provided a large piece of delicate white nylon and a number of chiffon scarves. The children danced with them, felt their texture, and finally composed a short dance sequence, drawing their movement patterns and writing about the scarves. This was one dance pattern drawn in coloured pastels on a large sheet of paper:

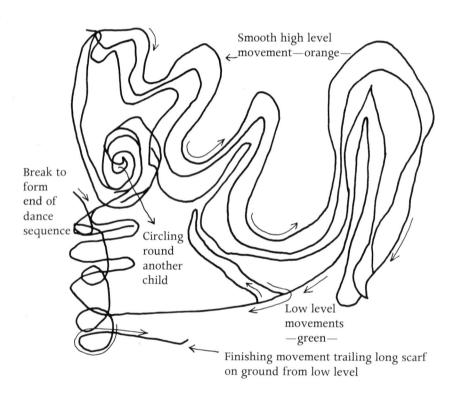

Smooth high level movement—orange—

Break to form end of dance sequence

Circling round another child

Low level movements —green—

Finishing movement trailing long scarf on ground from low level

The shapes the scarves made reminded the children of a great variety of things. One group listed them:

Scarf Dance

Dancing with clouds,
Birds, Kites, spinning tops,
Trampoline,
Waving, springing, Balloons,
Haunting, velvety, spooky,
Like a dream, hair newly washed,
Curling smoke from a cigar,
Angels' wings,
Leaves in autumn,
Cleanliness,
Brides and bouquets,
Bubbles,
Roundabouts,
Catherine wheels.

Individually, Nataszar wrote:

Soft like a dress
like clouds in the sky
Snow coming down
Sheep in the hills.

And Alastair:

I think . . .
it is like the sea,
ghosts angry throwing things about.
Africans in the scarf
Roundabouts, round and round
They are blue
Hold it against the light and the
Dark blue is light rinded (rimmed)

Seeing their enjoyment, the teacher later introduced different textures—silk, taffeta, hessian, blanket—for them to feel with their hands and feet and to dance with. They danced round and under the materials.

111

On another occasion the children listened to the record of *The Ritual Fire Dance*, and each child interpreted the music in his own way. Some danced as if they were actually in the fire and became flames or flickers.

When the teacher read an extract from Gerard Manley Hopkins:

> . . . Pale water, frail water,
> Wild rash and reeling water . . .

the children rendered the words as they wished. Some were in the water, while others became a flowing river, a trickling brook, or a waterfall.

After all these sessions some children were stimulated to write about or paint their impressions.

When the teacher decided to try out shadow dancing, with the help of a spotlight, she found that very young children found it difficult to concentrate on their shadows independently of their bodies. When the spotlight changed colour, they responded to being in the colour rather than making their black shadows move, but they had very definite ideas as to how the

113

different colours should be shown in movement, and many experiments were carried out to music made or chosen by the children to represent colour. In the next chapter we shall go into more detail about the relation of colour and music.

We always tried to ensure that these experiments did not detract from the basic qualities of music, movement, art and drama. Each discipline, although integrated with the others, must be carried out to the best of the child's ability. As with all teaching, we tried to find the right opportunity for introducing the situations which stimulated creative activity, for, as Dr. Bronowski said, "Every animal leaves traces of what he was: man alone leaves traces of what he created."[3]

References

1. R. Laban. *Modern Educational Dance*. Macdonald and Evans, 1963.
2. *Movement—Physical Education in the Primary Years*. Department of Education and Science, H.M.S.O. (London 1972), p. 119.
3. Dr. J. Bronowski, *The Ascent of Man*. Published in *The Listener*, p. 605, Vol. 89, No. 2303.

CHAPTER 6

Music and Language Development

We hope that we have shown that one of the primary aims in teaching music to children of the first school is both to help them to listen to and hear music, and to give them an awareness of sound and its framework, which is silence. This awareness leads to the appreciation of specific rhythms and patterns of music, and from this it is an easy step to give to these patterns some kind of written form, so creating a link between hearing sounds and representing them in visual form.

If we consider the following statements in D. Moyle's book *The Teaching of Reading* we see that the basic activities involving the most simple musical experience are of great help in learning to read.

"The mind must be able to interpret the stimulus received upon the retina and associate it with a sound value which has meaning within the individual's experience."[1]

"The eye traverses the line of reading material by a succession of movements and pauses."[2]

"All reading has its basis in the recognition of symbols,"[3] and so reading is seen as "turning the collection of symbols seen upon a piece of paper into talk".[4]

Learning to express themselves

Our children, in their experience of music learn to connect symbols with sounds and to recognise the rhythm of sounds and pauses. Visual, auditory and motor powers which must be developed for reading are used in musical activities. They have to learn visual discrimination, left to right orientation, and visual memory.

115

Children learn to communicate by sounds and the spoken word before they can write. So we talked about sounds to the children, helping to enlarge their vocabulary and encouraging them to speak coherently and fluently about their musical development before any written form or score was attempted.

Some 4 + to 5-year-old children were talking about what they liked doing in summer time. Their teacher wrote down some of their sentences and sounds which were incorporated on a frieze in their classroom music area. Some had been for a walk in the country by a stream. Here are some of their comments:

We walked gently over leaves, shuffling along, *shff, shff*.

a gentle breeze blowing through the tall grass and trees *shshsh, swish, shoo.*

birds moving, flying and singing, *trp, trp, tck, tck, cr cr, flp, tweet, tweet, cuckoo, cuckoo.*

a woodpecker *bbb, jjj, ttt, rrr, br br.*

animal noises in the long grass and bushes *se se, shff, trrch, trc, ee, ee, whsh, whsh,* a rustling, shuffling, scraping sound.

children laughing *aah, ahah.*

footsteps on the soft ground *plff, chk, sh sh.*

walking across a wooden bridge, *stamp, plomp, plonk, conk.*

the stream makes a tinkling sound *trk, trk, wsh, wsh, spish, spish*

children throwing stones into the water *plist, plist, plit.*

Other children had been to the sea and thought about the fish there. Their descriptions were written on the shape of a large fish:

striped fish
spotted fish
gold fish, silver fish
swimming happily

sad fish, happy fish
funny fish, odd fish
fat fish, bumpy fish
darting in and out

strange fish
fierce fish
huge fish
small fish
at the bottom
of the sea

This writing was surrounded by pictures of all kinds of fish with the imagined sounds in the air-bubbles around them.

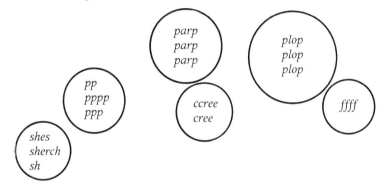

We would like to emphasise that music areas in the classroom should not be untidy neglected odd corners; they should be well-thought out, interesting and often changed to suit the themes which the children are currently discussing. In this music area, the walls were carefully lined with colourful frieze paper, and there were delightful mobiles of fishes hanging from the ceiling as a backing for some of the instruments. Shelves made from drama blocks or pieces of wood were covered in clean bright hessian, with well-written cards placed near some selected instruments in case the children needed some stimulus. For example, beneath the frieze of sounds and pictures of woods and the stream there was a card written by the teacher,

Can you make a tinkling sound like a stream?
which instrument would you use?

117

There were Indian bells and pieces of junk material near by. Other cards asked,

Can you make animal sounds?
A lion roaring
A dog barking
What other animal sounds can you make?

Can you make music?

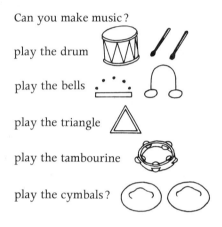

play the drum

play the bells

play the triangle

play the tambourine

play the cymbals?

Can you make these sounds?
children laughing
birds singing
wind blowing
waves splashing

The words were all used regularly in their reading and the children helped each other to understand the questions or asked the teacher if necessary. If they wished, they put up their own work in the music area, and added simple relevant reference books on any material or instruments they may have had at home.

In this school we are constantly directing our energies to help children to improve their reading and develop their spoken and written language. We encourage them to listen to sounds and observe what goes on around them, and in this way the children learn to express what they hear, see and feel so that they will write clearly and concisely in later life.

John, a small child of five, was talking to his teacher about the rain and she wrote down his phrases:

I like the rain because it makes my hair wet. Rain is drops of clean water. Rain comes from the clouds and clouds come from aeroplanes because the smoke makes clouds. The rain goes to sea to make it bigger and then the tide goes out. The rain falls through the gaps of the trees.

Their ideas grow from their experience. A group of 5 + to 6-year-old children found in the music area an interesting stone which had been brought to school to demonstrate what sounds stones made when rubbed against each other. Their discussion led on to this description of the stone. A new word "glissering" was invented by one of the children and left in the description.

A stone
Glissering and sparkling
Shining and glittering
Stars of gold
Diamonds like Mum's ring
Light and bright like the sun;
It has colours shining, like water
running over a stone
Delicate speckles,
White, black,
Grey and bumpy
It looks as though it has been
polished into rectangles
It must have come from mountains
or rock shells

The child's happiness and success or failure in the first school depends largely on his effective acquisition of adequate linguistic skills. His language development must be based on wide experience, plenty of opportunities for conversation, both listening and talking, and spontaneous and structured play.

Only then will his intellectual growth and skill in thinking develop simultaneously. When pursuing the creative activities we have described, the children develop various forms of thinking, which include reasoning, intuition, creativity, memorisation, and judgement. If the child has the opportunity of

119

performing these mental operations at his own level, helped by personal enthusiasm, then his thought processes and performance will probably reach the highest level of which he is capable.

When the child's creative energy is released, it becomes obvious that he does not compartmentalise the various ways in which he can express himself. The child appears to see painting, making music, writing or creating a dance as complementary rather than mutually exclusive. Sometimes the music precedes the language, as when the child's ideas are perhaps still in the process of formation, or when his thoughts present a difficult problem. Just as the young child will use an appropriate gesture or facial expression to convey his meaning when he cannot find the right word or phrase, so our children often experiment with sounds before choosing suitable ones to construct a coherent musical shape or pattern.

A class of children aged from 5 + to 6 years old were told Oscar Wilde's story *The Nightingale and the Rose*, and they were very taken with the quality and power of the bird's song.

> So the Nightingale sang to the Oak-tree, and her voice was like water bubbling from a silver jar. . . . Then she gave one last burst of music. The White Moon heard it, and she forgot the dawn, and lingered on in the sky. The red Rose heard it, and it trembled all over with ecstasy, and opened its petals to the cold morning air. Echo bore it to her purple cavern in the hills, and woke the sleeping shepherds from their dreams. It floated through the reeds of the river, and they carried its message to the sea.

They talked about it after hearing the story, choosing words such as "delicate", "silvery", but still felt they had not pinpointed the movement of the song's outpourings. Then suddenly one boy pointed to a pale spiral of a wood shaving, hanging from the ceiling in the music corner: "That's what it is like." As they failed to find an appropriate verbal symbol, they had taken the abstract notion and identified its qualities in a physical object.

The witches come out to play

At other times the children work from a more concrete starting point and use words quite happily, later elaborating their

120

expression with the appropriate music or sounds. One class of 34 children, aged from $5\frac{3}{4}$ to $6\frac{1}{4}$ years, together described in writing a frieze which showed witches and wizards coming out to play in a cave, where there was a spell pot and a witch's prison. The children began imagining aloud what the cave was like, and what the witches used for spells. Simon said "The cave would be deep, go back a long way, and echo," and Nicola added, "The witches have all spell things lying on the floor, and in the corners." Eventually the class teacher decided to get them to write a description of the witches coming out to play. The children worked together, all giving their own impressions of what would happen. The finished description, written down by the teacher, culminated in the witches' spell-making, since the children felt this echoed the finished frieze.

The Witches Come Out to Play

The cave is full of dirty animals, cobwebs and ants and you can hear echoes of your footsteps; pieces of rock would fall and make it echo like stones falling on tiles. It smells of witches, like a horses stink. It smells ferny, smoky and powdery from the cooking pot. First of all a big round eye floats along near to you, then you see a pointed hat bumping up and down. Then you see another dull red eye with pointed corners, and the eye comes towards you and you see the whole body coming near to you, but it is not like our bodies, it is disjointed, a bit like a skeleton.

The cave lights up and then the witch calls with a sharp, siren sound to the other witches and wizards. They bring by their magic into the cave, spiders, cobwebs, worms, stinging nettles and pieces of old paper left lying on the ground. Wispy the witch tells Sapaa the wizard to begin the spells. They put poison and powder and skeletons and spiders' blood and dinosaurs' neck into the pot. They look ugly and evil and their mouths go skew whiff. They make spiky laughter. Some sway and swish from side to side slowly and others stamp and jerk their bodies.

Later the children, working together again, wrote a spell for the witches to chant.

A week later, the children decided that they would like to use the witches for their class assembly. When the teacher read the description through again, it was obvious that the children felt an extra dimension was needed, as it was taking shape as a short piece of drama. They felt that if speech and movement could be highlighted by appropriate sounds, then the whole dramatic presentation would be strengthened.

Once again the teacher read the piece through slowly, the children stopping her when they thought a sound would add to the narrative. Nicola stopped her at "pieces of rock would fall and make it echo like stones falling on tiles". The children were initially puzzled as to what sound to use. Several ideas were put forward for an echoing sound but none seemed just right. All the suggested sounds were rejected by the class because they did not echo or for not being interesting enough. The children were feeling towards the tone or "colour" of the sound and were exercising a concentrated perception in their judgement.

John, looking around the room, suddenly said, "We could use stones", and fetched some from the weighing table. Children tried dropping them on a table one by one and this was hailed as fairly successful. They decided not to drop them too regularly, and at last Conrad grabbed the enamel bowl exclaiming "This is best to drop them on", and when a child dropped the stones at intermittent intervals on the upturned enamel bowl, the class were satisfied.

The class felt that sounds were needed when the witch's hat bumped up and down. Caroline tried hitting a chair with the flat of her hand, then with the tips of her fingers. It was considered too monotonous. Jane offered to help by alternately hitting the floor, but the sounds were too similar. Looking round, she saw an earthenware flowerpot hanging from the ceiling in the music area, and hit it with a wooden beater while Caroline continued to hit the chair seat. These differently pitched sounds appealed to all; perhaps partly because the children had again pinpointed a physical, concrete difference in the sounds, since the level of the suspended flowerpot was appreciably higher than that of the chair seat, physically as well as in sound.

The teacher's control of the class

The children regarded anything and everything as a possible instrument with which to make a sound which would enhance their narrative. Their acceptance of what some would consider unconventional and therefore inappropriate material pinpoints a problem central both to creative work in language and to creative work in music and movement. In *Hear and Now*,[2] John Paynter states that creative music work is sometimes seen as an activity for the "un-musical", while "the real thing" is left to those who can play an instrument and deal with crochets and quavers! He continues to say that many books on Primary music do not seem to recognise that music, like other arts, has basically very simple raw materials, and these are sounds. Since these raw materials can be explored and shaped into musical ideas, the child must just begin by finding out what he can do with the basic material. Nowadays this principle is recognised in the teaching of art, but it is often forgotten in musical and language work, even though there may be some lip service paid to it and a recognition in theory.

In work in music and movement the child is encouraged to produce ideas and deal responsibly with situations. But laissez-faire principles are not admissible. As with the language work in this school, the musical activities are characterised by teaching, and do not belong to the "capillary attraction" school of thought.[3] This has been explained as the idea of "putting children in the way of reading and spelling",[4] so that these will be assimilated through their pores. While we believe in providing exciting classrooms and surrounding the child with equipment which gives him the opportunity to explore and to think for himself, we also ensure that this means of discovery is co-ordinated with systematic tuition and an informed classroom practice.

At a time when emphasis is placed in the colleges of education on the need for the child to wish actively to learn, the part of the teacher in providing the conditions within which the child can make progress is sometimes underestimated. "Don't cram" is sometimes interpreted as "Don't teach". A teacher or student may think that since a child learns at his own pace, and in his own time, it is unnecessary to teach him, as he will "pick it up" when he is ready for it. The importance of motivation in learning is great, but it is not the only factor. He needs properly graded experiences of the meaning of symbols in order to learn to read, and it is part of the teacher's skill to provide these experiences in an orderly and controlled sequence.

Similarly, the teaching of music can and should be controlled, whether the class teacher considers herself unmusical or not. She can organise the music corner so that different topics are covered one after the other. For one half-term she may collect a variety of objects to help the children develop an understanding of pitch. Probable items for inclusion could be assorted bottles, to be filled with various levels of water; an enamel bowl to be struck with different beaters; washing-up liquid containers which can be filled with different sized objects of various weights; nails of assorted lengths and flowerpots of different sizes to be suspended and struck; elastic bands of different length and thickness to be plucked.

When the children have experimented with the sounds and decided which objects make high and which make low sounds, they can then sort these into groups. Later they can work towards a graduated order of pitch. The child can put the object which in his opinion makes the highest sound at one end of the line, and work through the objects till he can place the one with the lowest sound at the other end. Various groupings will be possible, since an enamel bowl hit with a wooden beater may make a different kind of sound from that struck with a metal one.

This exploration must be watched over by the teacher. She cannot hopefully leave them to perpetual *ad hoc* discovery. Sometimes music making is valuable for its provision of first hand experience, and the children's activity is worthwhile for just what is happening at that moment. At other times a teacher can step in and ask why hitting a long nail sounds different from hitting a short one. She can urge them to listen to their sounds, and try to fit them together to make a sound pattern. She might say, "You've got a good sound there, but can you make it different? Keep making that sound, but see what *you* can do to change it somehow. . . . Tell me how you've changed it."

The teacher can construct an activity in which she asks the children to use their voices to explore pitch, and she can then follow ideas which will be suggested by the children. Always there will emerge ideas and interest in the way one can use a voice.

Any class teacher can help children who are starting school to use their teeth, tongue and vocal powers as a way to begin music. Nursery rhymes, correct breathing and diction for singing, sol-fa are all important, but they are not enough. Vocal work

124

does not consist of just singing, but of using the voice as an instrument, another creative medium, which often needs to be associated with movement.

In a reception class, there were some boys who thought that it was "cissy" for a boy to sing songs. But when they were asked to use their voices as instruments, a very noticeable change took place. When sounds rather than paint were needed for weather effects on a rain frieze, these boys were among the first with ideas, and commented very soon that *zt, zt* would sound a harder rain than *pt, pt*. When the whole frieze was "sung" they participated happily.

It can be seen that one of the main principles behind our teaching is that if given opportunities children will take them. It is often difficult to predict what will happen, but if the activity is to be interesting the child should be personally motivated, not continually spurred on by the teacher's unchangeable plans. However, a teacher can often see possibilities in the work which the children are only half aware of. In the construction of a poem there is an inevitable process of selection, since poetry is a concentration of emotional and intellectual expression, and their half-formed ideas have to be drawn out by questions from the teacher, so that other children can elaborate to achieve the necessary "tightness" of expression for poetry. If an adult is being honest about children's creative work, then she cannot put ideas into their heads and shape them herself. She can lead the children towards a critical evaluation of their own suggestions and of the form into which they can be put. There is no reason why this should not work with 5- and 6-year-olds, as well as with the older child. Children of this age exhibit a surprising degree of sensitivity and an awareness of the suitability of their ideas and the sounds appropriate to them. In this work the contents of the situation are defined mainly by the children, while the teacher ensures that they are working and thinking to their fullest capacity.

More experiments with sounds

We believe that every encouragement should be given to children to discuss and impart their ideas as clearly as possible to others, so extending their command over language. This can happen also in the development of music.

Once a group of about 30 children from 5 + to 6 had been talking to their teacher in the music workshop about sounds and patterns of sound in the house, "because every sound makes a pattern, doesn't it?"

"Which sound did you choose, Lisa?"

"A dish-washer," said Lisa. "There are jets of water going on like this, *sh, shish, shish, shish, shwish, shwish.*"

The rest of the children joined in to make a rhythmic pattern of sound.

"What did you think, Robert?"

"When you chopped up sounds it sounded like a car wash—like a sound when you're breathing outwards very hard—*uhuuh, uhuuh, uhuuh, uhuuh.* That's a car-washing machine sound and if we all do it together it will sound more powerful," replied Robert. Again all the children joined in.

"A washing machine—the washing noise goes round and round *oom shuuuih shuish shuish,* but when the spin dryer comes on it makes a *zwuuu-zwuu-zwuur* sound (a low sound made very quickly and continuously with the voice going up and down a little).

"I can make a vacuum cleaner sound, *zweeeer zweerer zweeer.*"

"I can hear a kettle whistling like this," said Michael. "It starts slowly whistling on a high note, then when Mum turns it off it goes like this *ssuiooohoooh* and it ends softly in some steam."

"I know," Jane volunteered, "an electric toothbrush. It goes up and down, *zwee zweeu zweer, seeee seeee*" (a fluctuating sound, high like a bee).

"A door bell—*ding dong ding dong.*"

"I've got an electric bell," said another, "*zzzz zzz zz zz*" and a telephone, *prr prr, prr prr, prr prr,* and some in hospitals go *ddd ddd derr derr,* in a dull flat sound."

The children suggested many more sounds, each adding information as their enthusiasm mounted. They decided to listen for other sounds at home and talk about them during their next session.

A number of children in this group had parents or brothers and sisters who played or were learning to play some musical

126

instruments at home, and after discussing the sounds they made, they went on to talk about what the instruments looked like. Some of these children wanted to draw and write about them in a very simple way. Robert, although hardly able to write a sentence, was so keen that he insisted that the teacher wrote down the words so that he could copy them. He drew a saxophone, guitar and recorder and attempted to write:

We have these at Home.

Karen wrote:

This is my sister alison Playing her Oboe.

and drew a picture underneath with a shower of crotchets and quavers coming from the instrument.

Michael drew a guitar, trumpet, drum and piano, with their names written underneath them, followed by this sentence,

My Mummy and daddy play My daddy on the guitar and mummy on the trumpet.

We were impressed by the children's eagerness to write and the satisfaction it gave them to have written so much. They were helped with spelling when they asked. When very young children are writing about their original experiences or ideas, they are keen to put down their flow of words on paper without too much attention to spelling and punctuation, but we do emphasise that they should subsequently be helped so that they crystallise their ideas and have the chance to correct and re-write their work.

Andrew wrote under his drawing,

I like music becos you can dror the choon with a pencil and soft music can send you to sleep

Stuart's comments and his music were written like this:—

I like music and I like to Hum I do like Huming Because I can play Music I can sing to Music and I can Hum to Music I do like Music

127

and I can play Music like this

I can sing that like this

taa   ta té   taa

These examples and those of the other children were stuck into a big book which they had made. We leave such books about the classrooms, libraries or corridors because we find that children are always interested in reading the writing done by their peers and by children from other classes. In another book, *Poems about Instruments*, made by a group of six-year-olds, each child had chosen an instrument they liked to play and drew a description of the shape and components of the instrument and also of the sound it made: This is what some of them wrote.

Fiona:

The Tambourine

It is twirly
And sort of whirly
You can scratch it
You can bang it
enything works on
      a
Tambourine.

Mark:

The big drum

loud
deep
hard big sound
makes me think of
a big band.

Simon:

Indian Bells

Clickety clack go the horses hooves
and ding dong go the Church bells and
the foxes howl and fritense People

A child's ability to perform an action is usually in advance of his ability to explain what he is doing. This applies as much in describing a musical activity as any other.

Under the general theme of Shape, ideas in both mathematics and language were developed together with music. Some six-year-old children prepared a piece of work in which they used the sounds of instruments and choral speaking to illustrate the character of the shapes they described. One child described the shape. Two groups were involved in a two-part chant, and a third group accompanied it with their instruments:

1. (To Hands rubbed round and round a tambour and drum)
    whilst chanting the words "Round and Round and Round"
    A circle is smooth and whirly,
    A circle is smooth and whirly.
                                    (cymbals)

2. (Introduced by three sets of 4 strong beats on a large
    inverted beer can)
    A square has four even sides,
    and pointed spiky corners.
    It is straight (1 strong drum beat)
    And strong (2 strong drum beats)
    And not at all wobbly.

3. Short—long ⎫
    Short—long ⎪ (sounds tapped on
    Short—long ⎰ block = short—drum = long)
    Short—long ⎭

    A rectangle is long and narrow,
    Tall and thin,
    Straight and stiff like a wooden soldier.

    (4 brush beats on a snare drum.)

    Chorus Tinga-linga-ling ⎫
              Tinga-linga-ling ⎬ (to Indian Bells)
              Tinga-linga-ling ⎭

Other shapes dealt with by the children were a triangle, a star and a cross. They finished off with a chant and music combining all the different shapes.

On another occasion the teacher asked them to write down what was conjured up in their minds when various regular shapes were mentioned, after which they read aloud what they had written. Here is what some of them wrote:

> I closed my eyes and I thought of a circle. I saw a pool, biscuits and a record. I thought of a stabiliser wheel.

> I thought of an old fashioned cart wheel. it was a brown soggy one. left in a puddle it was a cart wheel, a Big one. with thick spokes going to the middle.

> A prickle on a holly leaf reminds me of a triangle.

> The roof of our classroom is triangular.

References

1. D. Moyle, *The Teaching of Reading*, Ward Lock Educational, p. 38.
2. Ibid., pp. 38–39.
3. Ibid., p. 104.
4. Ibid., p. 23.
2. J. Paynter, *Hear and Now; an introduction to modern music in schools* (Universal edition, 1972), p. 10.
3. M. A. K. Halliday's phrase; see D. Mackay, B. Thompson, P. Schaub, *Breakthrough to Literacy, Teacher's manual* (Longmans, 1970), p. 77.
4. M. Brearley (Ed.), *Fundamentals in the First School* (Oxford, Basil Blackwell, 1969), p. 61. Also see description of "teacher-counsellor" by V. Southgate and G. Roberts, *Reading— which approach?* (University of London Press, 1970), p. 26.

CHAPTER 7

Music, Colour and Language

Colour and music

Each classroom in the school has a chosen colour, and the Red Class made a *Book of Colour*. It started with such pictures as a red flower, fire engines and a pillar box together with a composition of words and music entitled *The Red Song*.

The Red Song

Red is a happy colour
It makes me feel so merry
Red is a happy colour
All day long.

Red is a shiny colour
It makes me feel so pretty
Red is a happy colour
All day long.

When I see a pretty poppy
Red in the morning sun
It makes me feel so pretty
All day long.

Red is a dangerous colour
Fire engines in a hurry
Traffic lights showing danger
All day long.

131

This was sung to the following tune in C. Major:

The Red Song

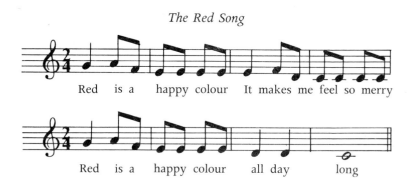

Red   is   a   happy colour   It makes me feel so merry

Red   is   a   happy colour   all day   long

We found that music and colours were closely related in the children's minds. A group of six-year-olds produced the following sounds which they felt represented the colours they spoke about.

To regular double beats on a drum they said:

x   x x Purple   x x Purple   x x Purple   x x
drum

Purple is my favourite colour
If I feel purple I run fast
We have purple flowers in the Autumn
And grapes and plums are purple too
x x   x x   x x   x x

To low notes on the xylophone—with regular beats on the drum all the way through:

Black

I feel sad, I feel horrible,
I feel frightened when I look at black
My black shoes have lines and
Holes in the middle of the lines

x   x   x   x   x   x

132

To Indian bells:

White

White makes me think of clouds and flowers,
It makes me think of chalk and polar bears.
I have got white hair. I like that.
I like my Mum in her white dress and
ribbons.

To notes on a recorder:

Blue

Blue is in the rainbow
Blue is in the sky
Blue sea, blue wool
Blue curtains
Blue makes me feel like laughing.

This work ended with a full orchestra of tunes from the bells, drums, recorders and xylophone.

The teacher had read to the class a poem by Christina Rossetti called *What is Red?* and the children felt moved to make up some music to this. When they were satisfied with it they made a tape recording in which they read the poem whilst instrumentalists played the accompaniment. They liked to hear themselves on the tape.

Another class of six-year-olds had produced a large book entitled *Through the Rainbow*, in which they pasted paintings, writing and pictures of the instruments and sound patterns which they thought went with the colour. Here are some of their remarks.

Yellow is jumpy, spotty, light and airy

Claire:

I like to play at the sea-side. I dig in the yellow sand and make sand castles sometimes it is soft and crumbly and I have to mix it with water

133

Lee said:

Violet is a quiet sleepy and gentle. This was illustrated by a pattern in violet paint.

Violet is played on the xylophone.

David wrote:

Indigo is spiky sharp and dark.
(There was a painting in indigo to illustrate this remark.)

Indigo is played on the triangle.

We found that quite often music influenced the children to use colour for expressing their feelings when records were being played.

One day some children were painting in a music workshop session whilst another group were playing records. The music teacher turned to see one boy moving by his easel to some African music, with brush in hand. He was making sweeping movements over his paper. Taking a closer look at his work, she saw that Warwick had painted a lively, intricate and colourful pattern in bright red, brown and greens interwoven with yellow and deep blue. These colours were extraordinarily like the bright colours that are so beloved of the African people.

As a result of this "sonic palette" she asked some other children to paint to different kinds of records. One was of an Air from Bach's *Suite No. 3*. What they painted was very representative of the style of the music.

This is Richard's picture:

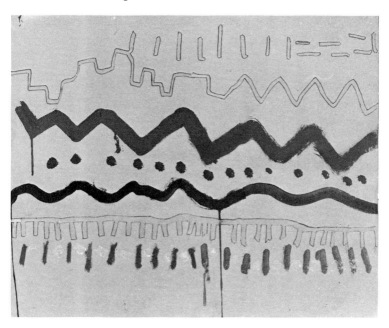

The *Polovtsian Dances* by Borodin produced an entirely different result. There were strong movements in black, dark

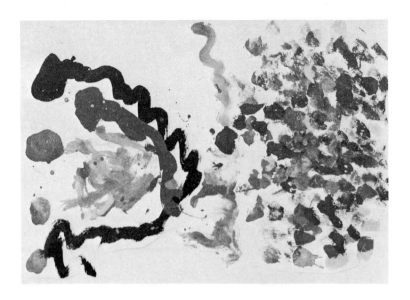

brown and dark green-blue at the left of the paper, and there were strong brush marks in dark browns, blues, greens and reds at the right.

The finished picture showed strong emotional feelings coming through, and gave movement to the painting and represented the child's reaction to the mood of the music.

Sounds and writing

There was one child of 6 + who enjoyed making sounds on any instrument but had not the slightest inclination to write anything down. Even when pressed firmly to do so, he would, and could, only form the simplest sentence. One day there was a shower of hailstones.

He said to his teacher, "I can make the sounds on a tambourine".

When he had made them the teacher said, "I wonder what those sounds would look like if you wrote them down?"

He answered, "I'll tell you all about it if you like", and eagerly he sat down and wrote:

                    (fell)   (ground) (pattered)
One day the hailstones fll on to the   grad   pat

    (melted)   (melted)
on and   melk | | | | ||| |||| and   melk   ⌒⌒⌒⌒

    (jumped fairly)
and   jup   feli (high and) got   •|•|•|•|•| and I (saw the)

                            (made)
hailstones   ∴∵∴∵∴∵   and   med   on the grad and   ⋎⋎⋎⋎⋎

(suddenly)
   sali   has gon

He also drew a picture of the hailstones. After that breakthrough to writing on his own he never looked back, and his
reading improved as well. There is no doubt that the teacher was
perceptive enough to realise that the arrival of the hailstorm and
playing of the instrument stimulated the language.
The children in the 6 + to 7 + age range began to write in a
more sophisticated manner about the sounds they heard.
Jacqueline wrote the following which she accompanied on a
drum, whistle and chime bars:

Sounds of the Morning. (drum)

A man walking thud thud first very quietly then quite loud but
all the time thud thud thud thats one of the sounds of the morning.
A bird singing like a whistler tweet tweet a little priter (prettier)
sound two sounds of the morning. (whistle)

Sound of evening

getting quieter and getting darck evry (every)-thing getting quieter
evry-one going home the day is diying (dying) ping, ping, ping—

Chime bar doyg doyg doyg dong
Chime bar ping ping ping high and low

137

Jane's story:

There was once a good family and one night is was so cold that the dog howld (voice, *whowhooowhoooooooo*) and the wind howld (recorder, *100101*) and it was so cold the thunder rolled

Alastair O—:

I was walking to school. I heard a car *eeeee whirrrrrr*. I walked on some dry leaves *crackle crackle crackle crunch crunk! crunch*—! I came to a signpost I read it I heard a BANG! I looked around. I saw a car broken down I went on my way. It started raining

softly louder I closed the door slam!

When asked about the quality of the sounds of various instruments they wrote:

Alastair M—:

The drum

> Tap gentle
> Tap hard
> A half cord and half boat-rope
> You put round your neck
> 2 drum sticks
> light wood on it
> like a snare drum
> a deep low bellowing sound
> rool (roll) the drum-stick across the white
> It sounds like a pencil.

Timothy:

> The glockenspiel is smooth
> It sounds like bells high up in the church
> It sounds like sharks streaking out of
> the sea
> Fish swimming under the water
> Rocks falling from the mountain
> It is deep is high is heavy

138

Encouraging research

We find that the work done in all fields of music made the children wish to search further for information. They frequently came to discuss their discoveries with their teachers or each other. We have libraries in the classrooms, the main library and in the corridors and music area so that there are plenty of books at each child's level of understanding. We are constantly adding to the libraries, and use a simple colour code to show the main areas of interest.

Library books were constantly consulted as the children became more confident in their writing and research, and we found the quality of the work improved. Their descriptive words came more easily and the children were able to work more independently in their groups without so much reliance on the teacher. Whether this was a direct result of the sounds we had discussed and discovered in music we cannot really say at this stage, but we know that as their music developed side by side with language it has stimulated them to think carefully about their choice of words.

There were several groups of children of 6 + to 7 + working on the theme of Time, and the following examples are some of their thoughts:

Winter and Spring
Dark and light.
Winter
Brown, white, grey, black, red.
Cold, rain, winds howling
Snow,
Foxes crying, hunters hunting.
Frozen waterfalls
Skeleton trees, bare like pylons.

Spring
Yellow, green, pink, turquoise, gold.
Warm, melting, longer days.
Time for growing
Crocuses yellow and purple
Grass fresher, greener
Blossom, flowers blooming, trees in bud
Gay, green, sprouting
Birds whistle,
Baby animals are born.

A class of the same age took Summer as a wide topic. They looked at the changing countryside, brought in items of interest for display and discussion—an old bird's nest, the skin of a sloe-worm, a beautiful rose. These children are in the school annexe, where they have a stretch of grass behind the classrooms touched by woodlands beyond. Just down the road, past houses with colourful gardens, is open land and a stream. Here they listened to the sounds and had to decide whether they were associated with summer or just every-day sounds.

The children wrote down their ideas.

One group wrote:

Sounds of Summer

Laughing voices of happy children
Buzz of bees, the hum of mosquitos
Drone of the mower,
Click of shears
The cuckoo in the woods,
Songs of birds
Splashing of water in the paddling pool
Rain from the hose pipe
falling on thirsty plants
Ping of the tennis ball
Creak of the swing
Tune from the ice-cream van
The sea crashing on the rocks, lapping on the beach
What a multitude of sounds we can hear.

The library offered plenty of reading material and the children were encouraged to look at and bring reference books from home.

Another class of a similar age made a book *Out of Doors in Summer-time*.

Katrina wrote out the class poem:

The Sun

Sun in space
High in the sky
Shining on the world
Shining on us.
A golden ball
Burning

On fire.
Without you
We would die.

Another child wrote:

The Lake

Silver blue-green water
Dazzling in the sun.
Swans swimming
Ducks diving
Fishes fins—flapping
Bubbles rising to the surface
popping and floating.
Green weed
Swaying, waving
Down in the deep water.

Some older children from 6 + to 8 + were more sophisticated in their thoughts on Time. This is an example from their group writings:

Thoughts on Time

When you're bored, time goes slowly.
Time passes quickly when you're doing
something interesting or enjoying yourself.
Keeping time in Music.
Take time and take trouble
Wounds take time to heal
Medicines take time to work
Sugar and salt take time to dissolve.
After rain the ground takes time to dry
Snow and frost take time to dissolve
It takes a long time to build a house and longer to make
a road or a block of flats.
It takes time to mend things
It takes time to find things.
Time can mean "Now", "Long ago",
or "in the future"
Time can mean clocks and watches.
Time is slow, fast, quick, stop.
If the world stopped, everything would stop.

141

Time is a difficult concept for children to grasp both in music and in history. The book which this class made was very enlightening. It showed a wide grasp of the meaning as they wrote articles on dinosaurs, Vikings, Nelson, "Hurricanes of the Present Day", clocks, "A Day in My Life" and "Flying Machines of the Future".

One group effort was written about Dinosaurs which seem to have a hypnotic effect on children!

Seven metres tall
Big clumsy body, small brain
Heavy as three double-deckers
Scaly, hard rough skin, bumpy brownish grey
Long tail fat and bulging ending thin
small arms
Big clumsy feet trudging, staggering,
rocking side to side
Expression fierce, enormous eyes
Teeth big sharp fangs tearing flesh
THUNDER
A roar like a hundred lions
The ground shakes
Me frightened, trembling, terrified
A giant like a skyscraper.
Head bent, teeth ready, tongue licking lips,
grinning.
Running faster, faster
Panting, stumbling
HELP!

The school contains reference books on the lives of musicians, orchestral instruments and their development, and the children are free to use these in their research into music. Many of the older children made their own books of instruments and studied the lives of composers such as Schubert, Handel, Ravel. When we touched upon the history of music with the younger children we used the Ladybird Books 1 and 2 *History of Music* with others which are in the library.

It was often possible to link the history of music with topics that were current in the classroom. Once a class of children from 6 + to 7 + years were very interested in Tutankhamun, and we talked about the kinds of instruments which the Egyptians played.

A picture of *The Flute Player* in the music area provided an interesting talking point as the player looked to be very much the kind of musician who might have lived in those days. We found a book containing pictures of some of these instruments and the children drew and painted pictures of them to add to their classroom frieze.

On another occasion a group of children of the same age were interested in cave men. This led to a discussion on very early musical sounds, e.g. bows twanged to charm animals. The children became so interested in primitive instruments that they made a xylophone out of stones of different sizes, and strung elastic bands round their teeth to twang so that they could simulate the sounds made by the bows.

The lives of some of the favourite composers, especially their childhood stories, make the children aware of them as real people. One day the music teacher played a record of some music by Benjamin Britten. They were amazed to discover that he was still alive.

We also tried to demonstrate the national flavour of music. For those children who had been to Spain, Spanish music was easily recognised, but when someone chose to play *Capriccio Espagnol* it was rather complicated to explain that this was written by a Russian, Rimsky Korsakov!

At this stage the teacher thought it relevant to draw the children's attention to the fact that a good tune could be played in different ways. For instance, Bizet's *Carmen* could be heard in a jazz guitar version of *Carmen* by Barney Kessel; or the tune from Beethoven's *Choral Symphony* is now sung as a "pop" song by the Seekers (Golden City). Although we are interested in music and folk songs from other countries we never forget our heritage of English music. We have a wealth of English folk music and singing games which are easily adaptable to teach sol-fa.

India was the scene of the story during an assembly about OXFAM. We did some interesting research into Indian musical instruments, managing to obtain a recording of sitar music and some pictures of a sitar for the children to see.

Once the Headmistress brought back a shivro from Tunisia. It was an earthenware pot shaped to fit under the arm and covered with a skin diaphragm at one end. It was used as a percussion instrument, i.e. it was tapped by the hands in the manner of a bongo drum. John brought an African drum, made from an animal skin, and Jane brought us a balalaika, all of which interested the children very much.

One of our most interesting acquisitions was a medieval bowed psaltery. This stimulated the children's interest in medieval music and led them to the discovery of the harpsichord and virginals. We visited a local instrument maker with a few children who were studying the harpsichord, and he showed us the internal workings and outlined its history. To see and hear the actual instrument being played was of great interest to us all.

Planning assemblies

Every week a different class of children take their own assembly, the topic of which they usually choose and to which their parents are invited. This always involves music of some kind to express their theme, quite apart from the hymns they choose or make up. The music teacher always co-operated with the class teacher if help was needed in any way, perhaps with singing or recorder players.

One class had chosen Power as their theme and Nancy had written:

> I am the wind
> and the lightning
> and I am the sun
> and I am the leopard
> and I am the horse
> and I am a fat elephant
> and I am a lion
> and I am a gorilla
> and I am a panther
> and I am the king
> and I am the power.

This stimulated more writing and a group of children went into the music workshop and decided to write about "The Power of God" using instruments to illustrate each line of the reading. The result was recorded on tape:

144

Power of God made the earth
(drums beating)
Made the seas and the fishes
(water sounds, Indian bells, chime bells)
Made the sun and moon and stars
("twinkle, twinkle little star" 1st two lines on bells and Indian bells)
Made the animals
(two notes played at intervals up and down the xylophone) (thirds)
The power of God made me.
(Full "orchestra" of all instruments used)

This was a very impressive ending to the assembly theme, where the power—water, heat, great steam engines and rockets —had been illustrated beforehand in mime and drama.

Another assembly developed when the class was considering a possible theme of Out of Doors. The teacher brought some records to school, *Fingal's Cave* by Mendelssohn and the theme for the television programme, The Onedin Line. These records stimulated the children's discussions about the sea, and they made a large book on the subject with writings and paintings.

Deirdre, aged 6, wrote:

When I went to the sea, the bubbling waves crashed against the rocks and bounced off.
The foam bounced too!
It bounced on the blue sea, high and low, up and down, like white balls. The little waves danced till they got to the golden sand and went back to the blue sea. The sea looked like the sky, a dark blue with little white clouds.
When the fish swam underneath, they made tiny chains of bubbles that wriggled like a snake in the deep sea.

The children had also been thinking of explorers and people who worked out of doors. One child brought to school an old book which contained the story of Grace Darling. This story fired their imagination and they thought it would be interesting for their assembly. Together the children prepared some choral reading, and they used the record *Amazing Grace*, which happened to be popular just then, as their hymn, with the music played by the class recorder players.

This is the introduction to their dramatic performance of her experience, written by a group:

> Darkening clouds covered the sun
> The whispering wind grew restless
> And gathered itself together, until it became a
> Howling, screaming monster, blowing the
> waves into
> towering walls, spiralling, twirling, curling,
> crashing,
> Booming, splintering against the rocks
>
> Far out on the sea a ship called Forfarshire
> forced its way through the heavy seas
>
> Battered and broken, it was driven on to
> the rocks
> Creaking cracking scraking smashing it
> disappeared gurgling beneath the waves
> Struggling groaning and shouting for
> help—the crew leapt into the sea.

Sometimes during music sessions the children listen to records of light or serious music chosen by the teacher from the growing collection in the music workshop. Some music is recorded on tape and the children may listen quietly to this from headphones plugged into the tape recorder.

A class of seven-year-olds were discussing how they enjoyed making music and listening to it in their leisure time. Some of the children brought records from home to play in the classroom, and the teacher let them interpret the music as they wished in movement and writing.

The children made a frieze and a large book called *Listening to Music*. They included colourful paintings, dance patterns and descriptive writing. They listed the records in the front of the book:

Pomp and Circumstance—Elgar.
Peter and the Wolf—Prokofiev.
Waltz in D—Chopin

Junior Hits—L.P.
Swan Lake—Tchaikowsky.
Songs of our Heritage on Guitar—Duane Eddy.

Although some of the children had heard the *Swan Lake* music before and recognised it as the *Dance of the Little Swans*, others made their own interpretation.
This is Louise's interpretation of music from Tchaikowsky's *Swan Lake*, Act II

> The music is soft and flowing. It makes me think of leaves blowing in the breeze and I feel sleepy. I think of the waves rushing over the rocks. I feel cold. I feel as though I am blowing in the air. Suddenly, trumpets and horns come into the music. The hunters arrive with their hounds looking for foxes, and the hounds are searching for the scent. The fox has disappeared into the bushes. The scent has gone, washed away by the rain. A thunderstorm has blown up. There is great pandemonium.
> All the hounds gather in a muddled circle.

Underneath is a striking and colourful pattern of sounds from a flowing turquoise sequence to strong brush movements in orange, black and red interspersed with calm grey areas ending with busy terracotta circular movements.
Andrew wrote of *Pomp and Circumstance*:

> Pomp and Circumstance has two different kinds of music. In the loud part I see in my mind an orchestra with violins, double bass, trombone, trumpets and drums play a loud rhythm. I think of a lion at a circus roaring loudly. The part I like best is the quietest part and I can imagine butterflies fluttering in and out flowers and the bees collecting up the Pollen their movement is beautiful it is graceful gentle and slow.

The school's internal broadcasting system

We have recently developed an internal broadcasting system in this school. The Studio is in the Headmistress's study. We collect our news from each class and broadcast it at a set time each week. We also use music and stories or plays.

147

Each class in turn is responsible for collecting, editing and producing the broadcast. So far the children from 6+ to 7+ have been concerned with the organisation of the weekly sessions. Class-reporters are sent round the school and return with news which they have written down or which the children from other classes may have prepared. It is edited and, if the producer thinks it necessary, suitable music is provided to introduce the session.

The initial broadcast was very carefully thought out. The Turquoise Class was the first to produce a programme and they wanted to give the station a name. *Radio All-Sorts* was finally decided upon. They then felt that there should be a special signal and eventually decided to use the notes C and F (for Chandler's Ford, where the school is situated) to be played on the glocken-spiel.

C   C   F

As the internal broadcast system works only in the main building and the five temporary buildings near by, we record the news on a portable tape recorder, which can be taken to the Annexe. All this requires thorough organisation and the children are becoming quite adept at carrying out the necessary operations.

The first broadcast opened with the signal, and then Robert, the producer, spoke:

> This is the Turquoise Class making the first School Broadcast. We have chosen the name of this programme. We do hope you like it. The radio signal is made up of the two notes C and F standing for Chandler's Ford.
>
> Richard, Jonathan, Claire, Elizabeth and Warwick played their violins to a large audience at Mountbatten School (a local Secondary Comprehensive School) last Saturday.
>
> News from Green Class.
>
> Jacqueline, Judith, Naomi, Fiona and Natasha went to Mountbatten School on Saturday to take part in a "Music of Strings" Day. They played their violins. . . .

It was interesting to note that the first items of news were to do with music! This was certainly not mooted by the teachers.

Later news of a different nature was read.

The Pink Class have made fairy cakes this week. A few weeks ago they made ginger-bread men. They have talked about the nomads in the desert, the Eskimos and people who live in Spain. They have secret smelling pots in their classroom. They have a hamster called Slinky which is nice to play with. Their tadpoles are growing fat. They have a new clock shop. They have got a Yellow table which reminds us of Spring. They have made new sounds with newspaper and then drawn sound patterns so that they could play music again.

The Gold class are making bread. When it is ready they hope that there will be forty pieces. All the children made up a little poem about it. Something like this:
"When the yeast was dissolving and getting active and bubbly it looked like chewing gum, cement, bits of broken up land, magic weetabix with warm milk on it sinking mud or sand."
Mrs. R— has two fishes called Fishy and Foshy. She would like some water snails. If anyone has any please would they bring some?
Music News from Mrs. B—.
The Green and Red Classes have written some interesting poems about instruments, and the Red Class have drawn some lovely dance patterns. These are on display in the Music Room. Do go to see them.

Robert read a story which he had written called *Race against Time*. Then he went on,

Your news reporters this week were
Claire, Warwick, Robert F—, Jonathan, David, Jane, Robert S—, James, Richard, Elizabeth, Claire. Goodbye Everybody.
These are your news reporters tuning out:

There was never any shortage of news as there were ten classes in the school.
On another occasion the children of the Red Class broadcast the words and music to the following song. They had been talking about sailing.

Hum, Hum, Hum,
Sh-, Sh-, Sh-,
The sea is waltzing, the sea is waltzing,
The sky is blue, the sky is blue.
The Seagulls are singing to me and you—
All day, all day.

The sails are flapping, the sails are flapping,
The wind is full, the wind is full,
The waves are bouncy and happy are we
All day, all day
Hum, Hum, Hum,
Sh-, Sh-, Sh-.

We consider that the development of music and language side by side has enriched both the teaching and the children's learning. Aural training helped to develop the child's pleasure in the sounds of words and the rhythms which could be made with them. Pitch work helped aural discrimination and hearing ability in general. Pitch-pattern work helped in that most children recognise sentences, phrases or words by their general pattern before they recognise specific letters.

Music stimulates writing. Progress depends upon the ability and interest of the individual child, but we have found that there are no set tasks that must be learnt at a specific stage. We think that interest and enjoyment are the keys to learning, and that means that if our suggestions are followed every child can attempt and benefit from music.

"Written speech," says Vygotsky, "is a separate linguistic function, differing from oral speech both in structure and mode of functioning. . . . It is speech in thought and image only, lacking the musical, expressive, intonational qualities of oral speech."[1]

Our aim is to encourage children to read fluently, to write clearly and concisely, not only imaginatively but also accurately. We, as teachers, need to distinguish between the spoken and written word and we must take care that the good work done in oracy does not squeeze out interest in the written word. Competence in the former does not necessarily lead to competence in the latter. Written language is likely to display a greater complexity of structure and sophistication of vocabulary than would normally be appropriate in speech. Whereas speech is acquired more or less inevitably by the average learner, merely through exposure to a normal human environment, the ability to write seems to depend to a greater extent upon teaching.

We believe in providing a rich experience for the children, and part of this experience is music which has added to their language and given the children the joy and freedom to experiment with sounds and touch. In this way the children learn to stop, listen and look closely at the stimuli around them. Our aim is and has been, as George Eliot said, to "escape from all vagueness and inaccuracy into the daylight of distinct and vivid ideas".

References

1. Vygotsky, L. S., *Thought and Language* (translated by E. Haufmann and G. Vakar). MIT Press, 1962.
2. *The George Eliot Letters*, ed. G. S. Haight, O.U.P., 1954.

151

CHAPTER 8

Summing Up

This book has attempted to describe work in music, allied to movement, drama, art, and closely linked with expression, both oral and written, which has developed during the three years that the Headmistress has been in this school. It began, as experimental change usually begins, with a feeling of dissatisfaction with the existing work in music, which was based mainly on the percussion band and singing accompanied by the teachers at the piano. The classes were usually large and directed by the teachers in the traditional way, with words often learnt in parrot fashion. Frequently the children seemed to have no idea of the meaning of the words or the phrasing of the music, whilst the "band" gave little scope.

As we have already shown, the children began to break away from this pattern when we encouraged them to bring to school anything manageable that could make a sound. Some of the uses we made of their collection of items have been described in some detail, but what we do stress here is the electrifying effect which the experience had on the children who took part in the experiments.

They were found to be bubbling with enthusiasm, as sentences such as these spilled out. "I didn't half like banging on those tins," said one of the group as they poured into the playground afterwards. "You should have seen your face, it was all far away," said Richard. "I felt I was going to dance and I was all excited inside." "It made my body dance," and "Did you see Alison and Peter jumping when you went faster?" "Mrs. — didn't stop us either. . . ."

A torrent of emotion had been released which had as much to do with verbal expression and bodily movement as with musical experience. The new form of music-making had stimulated an awareness of sound which changed the children's outlook. They reacted to the sounds they made in different ways: by aggressive excitement, physical emotion, and a need to express their feelings in dancing. In talking to one another they showed their powers of observation and their ability to describe in clear sentences what was going on.

As time went on we gave them more opportunities to make their own sounds. There seemed to be no flagging of their interest, and this interest led to freer movement, a development in drama, a fresh approach to art and an improvement generally in reading, speaking and writing.

It became apparent that much creative work was taking place as a result of the children's own discoveries. Gradually, as we have seen, their activities became more sophisticated. They became more aware of differences between various sounds, and began to understand pitch and rhythm. As the work progressed, techniques emerged by which the children recorded the "music" they made by using various symbols. This development, of course, was closely linked with both art work and writing.

The children's sensitivity in several directions improved. They became aware of the need to press and pluck strings lightly or strongly, little fingers tapped elbows, knees, drums, floor or paper softly or loudly; they clutched beaters delicately or firmly; gongs, cymbals and dustbin lids were struck with varying degrees of force.

It became obvious that work of this kind did not demand a music specialist, but was within the capabilities of most teachers. The children's sensory and motor activities could be stimulated by the teacher's ideas, and each child could be helped at his own level, thus leading him to a fuller realisation of the quality of his own work.

Many teachers feel that they cannot sing, or even attempt to play a musical instrument. This assumption hardly holds water because once initial shyness is overcome practice and confidence usually ensures success. However, in reality, factors such as lack of time and opportunity make many infant teachers regard themselves as "non-musical", and they tend to shy away from any activities other than nursery rhymes and simple songs. We believe, on the other hand, that most infant teachers can tackle

153

music and explore its creative possibilities, producing results which are far from banal and helping children towards a mastery of the often exacting skills involved. We have found that those who have become interested in these experiments would never, at the outset, have thought they could be so successful. The very enthusiasm of the children has led them on. It has been proved that these musical activities could be used in other classroom spheres by a so-called "un-musical" teacher to keep up the interest of the children—whether they are slow and difficult or potentially talented.

While music teaching often demands a high level of competence from the specialist teacher, it can and should also complement all creative media used in class. Although expensive instruments stretch the child's skills and extend his enjoyment, the music potential of "junk" and everyday material need not be as limiting as many might think. We believe that

(1)　Music in its widest sense should not be the sole responsibility of one teacher in the school, who teaches it more happily than anyone else.

(2)　The teaching of music in our school underlines the belief that in a teacher-controlled situation, where respect and trust are mutual, learning is a pleasure to the child. Not one of our children has yet said, "I can't do music."

We have shown how the class teachers start with music work, which, supplemented by the specialist teacher's activities, leads the children to understand the ideas involved in their musical experiments. Their music becomes so clear to them that they often wish to remember it exactly, and to analyse its rhythm, pitch, tempo, dynamics, mood and style. This analysis occurs at different levels with different children, but one of the most exciting results of our music work is the way in which the children seem able to invent their own ways of writing it down. They seem to disregard difficulties and the results have not been imposed in any way by the teachers nor are they the result of suggestions.

The Headmistress, who has had a life-long and deep-rooted love of and interest in music, has throughout her teaching career made free use of this interest in movement, language development and the allied arts. After a term in her present school she wished to introduce these ideas and, when the opportunity arose

154

for a part-time appointment to the staff of a reading and language teacher, she made sure that the teacher appointed had some musical qualifications. The newcomer had little real ability on any musical instrument except the recorder, which she had not touched since school days, nor was she an experienced piano player. She had, however, a fully trained singing voice, could sing at sight and had a fundamental knowledge of musical form.

Given the opportunity to develop music along less formal lines throughout the school, the problem was, where to start? The first thing was to establish a music area in the school entrance hall, with a few conventional percussion instruments such as triangles, drums and cymbals augmented by a snare drum with brushes, a xylophone and bongo drums. Rolls of coloured corrugated paper were carefully placed to make separate bays for display areas. Record sleeves were arranged above the area where the record player was kept. As all the children saw the instruments at one time or another—going to assembly or out to P.E.—they asked innumerable questions about them and became excited about the display.

Eventually, at the beginning of the school year, when the numbers on roll were at their lowest, we were able to turn a small classroom into a music room where groups of children could explore sounds in a musical workshop. When numbers grew, this room had to be given up, and the work went on in the entrance hall.

Gradually other members of the staff began to show an interest in this experimental type of music. As time went on each teacher used some part of her classroom for experiments in sound and music and more instruments were added. A vital part of the teacher's role is to share in the experiences which the child enjoys and to share with other teachers each child's enthusiasm. In this way our kind of team teaching—which we call co-opera-tive teaching—both helps the child and extends the teacher's interest in sound. The discussions between teachers about their classroom projects were found to be both useful and inspiring.

The teachers presented many musical opportunities to the children, and at least four of them, for their own enjoyment, learnt to play the guitar at a course run at the local Teachers' Centre.

We wondered how the experimental work would affect formal

violin teaching, given by a teacher, with L.R.A.M. qualifications, who came to the school for an hour each week. At the end of a year's work with the children, she wrote down some of her impressions. She said that the atmosphere in the school was conducive to learning the violin. "Violinists, like greenhouse plants, need the right conditions in which to flourish. . . . The children are very responsive and eager to work very hard despite the usual technical problems every violinist faces. Some parents are always present at lessons (some even learn to play the violin so that they can help their children) and one father has become our resident pianist. The children are willing to put in the necessary practice at home with helpful parents."

The children who have violin lessons in the school have joined a junior orchestra in a nearby town and take part in concerts and rehearsals after school hours. Many parents have found that their initial interest has grown into a desire to participate. Several have taken up piano lessons again in order to accompany sons' or daughters' violin or recorder practice. Many have attended the violin lessons in the school and have brought their own violins out again. Parents and children have attended performances of opera, recitals, and orchestral concerts brought to the area by the local Arts Association. The local private teachers of instruments have waiting lists of children wishing to continue their music when they leave the school and a junior orchestra is planned for the area in the coming year. Music is an integral part of the assemblies which parents are welcome to attend.

Other parents came into school to accompany the children at the piano or to help to interest them in certain instruments which they play. Two parents found the time one morning to bring their instruments—a trumpet and a trombone. They played them to the children, showed them how they were made, and explained how the different notes were played. The children were enraptured.

Part of their conversation went like this—spoken by the parent with a trumpet:

"If I blow without putting the valves down leaving all the valves up (blowing note), the air just goes straight round there and straight out through there (pointing to relevant parts on the instrument) without going round any of the valves. If I put the valve down, the air goes down there, (again pointing to instru-

156

ment) into there and then round into that tube and out at the end, and that's how we play the note—making the tube longer by pushing the valve down. (blowing note)

"I'll show you what the valve looks like inside now. There it is, full of holes!" (Cries of wonder from the children.)

"Did you know that the longer the tube, the deeper the note?" (Some cries of "Yes" from the children.) "That's why a trombone is lower than a trumpet because it has a longer tube (pointing to trombone). And a tuba has a very low note, 'wumph' 'wumph', because it has a very, very long tube."

Other visitors to the school have brought such instruments as a 'cello and clarinet to play to the children. On one occasion Mike Garrick and his Jazz Group visited the school. This involved the piano, double bass and percussion, and it was very popular.

The children enjoyed having visitors to the school and discussing their work with them. One visitor to the school spent a long time with a group of about ten children discussing how their music evolved for an assembly which he had just attended. They talked about the kind of instruments the children enjoyed playing.

"I like playing the side drum, and I like the sound of the brushes," said Michael.

Visitor: "You were playing the side drum in assembly this morning weren't you? I thought you kept the rhythm going very well. What do you think you learn when you make up your own music?" he then asked.

"I learn rhythms and I learn how to play different tunes . . ." said Gregory.

"Would you like to make up any rhythm on your tambourine?"

Gregory's rhythm went:

"Can you do it again?"

He repeated it correctly.

The visitor asked "Do you think it is important to remember things?"

"Yes," answered Mark. "If you don't remember it wouldn't turn out the same."

Music has become part of the school life. The children see it in its place just as naturally as reading or mathematics. They appear to enjoy music and have become confident that they can take part in it.

We feel that we have helped many less able children to overcome their difficulties. Tom, aged 6½, had great trouble in controlling the finer movements of his fingers. He could not tie his shoelaces, do up buttons or pick up pins, but he was so determined to play the recorder that he overcame his difficulties and became very proficient.

Many children, unable to shine in other disciplines, have found in music an opportunity to do well. Some children who are extroverts have been labelled "naughty" at times and they have found outlets for their natural exuberance in music.

Only very recently, Alan, aged 6, who was a most difficult child and with whom we found it very hard to communicate, decided to join the recorder group. He discovered that he had a natural ability to blow and he made the sounds of the notes better than the others. He was very pleased with himself and went back to his class teacher ready to work hard. He has since developed an interest in drums.

The children are allowed to choose whichever instruments they wish to play. The girls play the drums or cymbals, which in the past have often been thought to be the prerogative of the boys, and boys play the Indian bells or tambourines or any other instrument.

Our theories are not wildly different from others which have already been put forward, but we have tried to show what has worked for us in our school. It has not been a case of "Chips With Everything" but a natural development of music in the classroom situation. We hope we have tried to help those teachers who have said to us "I don't know how to begin! Where do you start?"

In all, we feel that in no other discipline are the abilities of most small children so under-rated. They appear to have open and receptive minds which take in the essentials of musical sound in a clear uncomplicated way. They grasp the essentials unclouded by inhibitions or preconceived ideas of form. They

158

create real music full of life and innovations. Work with these young children has freed us from some of our own musical inhibitions and opened our ears to the modern composers.

Where, you might ask, do we go from here? How does this work develop with the older children? Children from 8 or 9 onwards need outlets for their creative potential.

In one Junior school a child of 9 years wrote a descant for a hymn, which was sung in assembly and at a Music Festival. Another class of children from 10 + to 11 have written their own scores and performed their music for cello, violin, descant, treble and tenor recorders and percussion. This same group wrote their own words and Chinese music for the story *The Emperor and the Nightingale* for a Music Festival.

A visitor to the school said that in his Junior School, music had been a vital source of inspiration through such records as *The Planets* (Holst), *Peter Grimes (Sea Interludes), Fantasia on a theme of Thomas Tallis, The Pastoral Symphony*, the music of Sibelius, Brahms, folk songs of all kinds (Joan Baez, Bob Dylan, Ewen McColl's *Dirty old Town*), blues and *The Good, the Bad and the Ugly*.

He has encouraged his children to make their own tape recordings of sounds. They have developed movement themes for a television performance, for services in a cathedral and assemblies. Sometimes the themes were an extension of creative work in the classroom. In our own school the Wessex Educational TV, which makes video tapes for colleges in the area, recorded several of the children's performances most successfully. These included *The Circus* and *The Fishermen*, pp. 95 and 96.

It can be seen from the preceding chapters that we believe that educating children for literacy should be interpreted in the widest sense. The first-school child should realise that communication is defined not only by reading and writing, but also by music and movement. If a teacher can view the child's self expression in the way we have described, then the process of education will surely be more alive, interesting and rewarding for both her and the child. Since the child finds no barriers to his self expression, his ideas should be communicated with increasing precision, clarity and vivacity. One result of this kind of work is that the very young child gains absolute confidence in his own creative powers in music once he has realised that his way of writing down the sounds is received with encouraging approval. We have found that a few children with educational difficulties—especially less able children with phonics—have been helped to improve their general educational performance and social adjustment because their confidence, boosted by music and movement work, has been increased. We feel therefore that the work we describe in this book may well be of particular value for the nursery school child, and for the child with educational difficulties, especially since the latter often finds verbal communication irrelevant or perplexing.

Music has been a common ground for developing relationships with children—no matter from what country or creed. We have made contact with children at our school from China, Japan, Holland and Brazil, through the common bond of sounds and musical experiences.

Recently, music has been used more in the treatment of autistic children and we wonder if the musical experiences we have described could be of use in building up a relationship with such a child and in increasing his confidence in his abilities. The problems of the culturally disadvantaged child have received a great deal of attention, with the result that we now realise that the more traditional idea of "literacy" is often alien to such a child. In this sphere, we feel that some practical research, using our ideas of music and movement, may well show some fruitful results.

It is an inescapable fact, however, that no educational schemes work by themselves. Their practical effectiveness obviously depends on the quality of the people who carry them out. Our ideas can only be translated into reality by teachers who feel enough confidence in themselves and in their children. We can only hopefully say to you "Put these ideas into practice—go on; try them."

References

1. M. Brearley (Ed.), *Fundamentals in the First School*, Blackwell, 1969, p. 127.
2. *Ibid.*, p. 129.

Appendix I

Musical instruments

We have shown that almost anything can be a musical instrument. When it comes to conventional instruments, we believe that one or two, well made and of good quality, are worth a host of cheaper ones. It is from these that a child will learn to discriminate between good and inferior sounds, as anyone who has heard, for example, a good cymbal against a cheaper version will understand.

A basic school collection might consist of:—

1. Tambourines
2. Different sized triangles
3. Maracas
4. Bongo Drums
5. Castanets
6. Chinese Beaters—different sizes
7. Tambour
8. Snare Drum
9. Small Drums
10. Bass Drum
11. Glockenspiels—Soprano and Alto
12. Xylophones—Soprano, Alto and Bass
13. Set of Chime Bars
14. Indian Bells
15. Cymbals of different sizes, but especially 18-inch.

Any other instruments which the school can obtain will be valuable. Very small children cannot, of course, play a 'cello, guitar or trumpet, but they can learn a great deal by experimenting with the sounds which they can get out of them, and much more by hearing them played by competent instrumentalists, who may be found among interested parents.

Bass sounds are often neglected in the Infant School, and a bass xylophone, or a double bass or 'cello can extend the range of the children's experience in sound and lend a new dimension to sound patterns.

Care of instruments

Children readily appreciate the need to take care of musical instruments, and will respond to the teacher who takes good care of them herself. Instruments should be cleaned regularly. Beaters should be kept in their pairs. Each triangle should have its string and a beater attached. Small children can be very frustrated if these details are not observed. The piano should be kept clean and tuned regularly.

Beaters

Various beaters offer opportunity for a wide range of tone colour. Recommended types are:—

1. Very soft—wool or felt head
2. Hard felt head
3. Felt head with wooden core
4. Hard head of wood or rubber, light
5. The same, heavy
6. Double-headed, soft and hard
7. Side-drum stick, nylon tipped
8. Side-drum brush
9. Timpani stick, wool or felt head.

Recommended records

A most valuable part of the music equipment is a portable tape recorder and a good record player. The following records are recommended:

The Nutcracker Suite—Tchaikowsky
A Midsummer Night's Dream—Mendelssohn
Dance of the Tumblers—Rimsky Korsakov
Comedians' Gallop—Kabalevsky
Magic Fire Music (The Valkyries)—Wagner
Ritual Fire Dance—Falla
Hungarian Dances—Brahms
Russian Sailor's Dance—Glière
The Pines of Rome—Respighi
Festivals—Debussy
L'Après midi d'un Faune—Debussy
Polkas & Dances by Strauss
The Swan Lake—Tchaikowsky
Carnival of the Animals—Saint Saëns
Peter and the Wolf—Prokofiev
Young Person's Guide to the Orchestra—Britten
The Sorcerer's Apprentice—Dukas
Pictures at an Exhibition—Mussorgsky
Polovtsian Dances from *Prince Igor*—Borodin
Night on the Bare Mountain—Mussorgsky
Cappriccio Espagnol—Rimsky Korsakov
The Hebrides—Mendelsshon
Overture The Magic Flute—Mozart
Overture The Thieving Magpie—Rossini
Music of Offenbach
Till Eulenspiegel—Richard Strauss
Overture William Tell—Rossini
The Firebird—Stravinsky

These are just a few suggestions. Popular music by Donovan, The Beatles, The Strawbs, Cat Stevens, etc. also have a place in stimulating language and movement, and giving pleasure. The teacher should always be listening for suitable music, preferably with good imagery and a strong beat.

Appendix II

Work cards are very useful in extending the exploration of music in the First School. The following cards are intended as suggestions which could be developed as the teacher sees fit.

The Music Area (Chapters 1 and 2)

You will need a selection of sound-producing materials other than conventional instruments, e.g.:

Closed tins, such as coffee tins, either empty or containing rice, small stones or sand.
Large marmalade tins with plastic lids.
Biscuit tins (rectangular or round, shallow or deep) with elastic bands of varying thickness stretched across them.
Smooth blocks of wood (offcuts—sandpapered to avoid splinters).
Sandpaper.
Bottles of varying sizes.
An assortment of shakers ("squeezy" containers and peas or macaroni).
Beaters of different kinds.
Paper—large sheets—paints, pastels, crayons.

1.

Find a tin

Find a beater

Draw the sound
you make

Suggestions

CARD 1

In the early stages, before any cards are used, it is important to encourage the children to listen carefully to the sounds they make and to describe them to the teacher or each other. Later they can be asked to draw a pattern to represent the sounds.

CARD 2

The bottles are filled with water to different levels to make notes of different pitch. These sounds can be related to conventional instruments and to the children's own voices.

CARD 3

Encourage the children to discuss the kind of sounds made by the smaller tins and those made by the bigger tins. Those from the smaller are higher in pitch than those from the bigger ones. Sounds also vary with the different beaters used. Carry on from here to produce sound patterns which can be reproduced in

165

2.

Find a bottle.

Blow across the top of it.

What kind of sound have you made?

3.

Find 2 tins:

A small one.

A big one.

Hit them.

What kind of sounds can you make?

drawings, paintings, or even danced to. (Chap. 5, p. 107.) Another possibility is to use them to reinforce their own stories. (Chap. 2, p. 24.)

For example:—

Write a story.

Use some materials to make sounds for your story.

Draw the sounds you have used.

Repetition of sounds assists reading development.

4.

Stretch some rubber bands across a box or tin.

Pluck the bands.

What do the sounds make you think of ?

CARD 4

Note that differing thicknesses and lengths of band produce different sounds or notes.

Relate to experiments in vibration. (Chap. 2, pp. 38–50.)

Auditory Discrimination and Aural Memory (Recall)

CARD 5

This experience can be extended to the playground where the children can listen to the sounds and draw them.

5.

Close your eyes.
Listen.
What can you hear?
Open your eyes.
Write down what you can
hear or describe the
sound to your friend.

6.

Listen for some loud sounds.

What are they?

How many can you hear?

Listen for some quiet sounds.

How many can you draw?

7.

Close your eyes.

Think about the sounds
you hear when you wake
up in the morning.

Draw them.

8.

Think of some sounds you
heard on holiday.

What kinds of sounds
have you heard at a party?

CARDS 6, 7, 8

The work could be extended to listening to the sounds which
the body makes, i.e. heart beats, breathing, and making sounds
with hands, feet, elbows, knees knocking, or the sounds which
the children could make on their bodies such as hands stroking,
clapping, beating. (Chapter 2, p. 34.)

169

```
┌─────────────────────────────────────┐
│                                     │
│  9.                                 │
│                                     │
│  Find some friends.                 │
│                                     │
│  Make your sounds into a pattern.   │
│                                     │
│  Sometimes have turns at            │
│                                     │
│  making your own sounds.            │
│                                     │
│  Sometimes play them together.      │
│                                     │
│  Make some quiet sounds.            │
│                                     │
│  Make some loud sounds              │
│                                     │
│  Make some quick quiet sounds       │
│                                     │
│  Make some quick loud sounds        │
│                                     │
│  Make some slow quiet sounds        │
│                                     │
│  Make some slow loud sounds         │
│                                     │
└─────────────────────────────────────┘
```

Patterns of Sounds

CARD 9

Patterns of sounds can be made and written down by the children (Chap. 3, p. 52.)

CARD 10

Newspaper, (Chap. 3, p. 54) tissue paper or any other kind of paper may be used to make sounds (flicking, patting, hitting, crumpling up). Considerable language development comes from these experiences. If you have a tape recorder many exciting sounds can be made to use as accompaniment to drama or movement.

170

10

Take a piece of newspaper.

What sounds can you make?

What does the paper sound like when you wave it in the air, or hit it with your fingers?

11.

Take some newspaper.

Find some friends

Make your own sound pattern.

Now join your friends

Decide which sound is to be played first.

Do not forget to make your sounds form a shape like this :—

loud

soft   soft

Choose a conductor and make your own 'Newspaper Orchestra'.

This work can lead to the children drawing the shape or pattern their sound makes, using the recognised symbols, e.g.

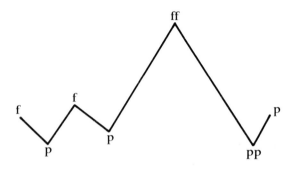

12.

On the Sound Frame

How many different kinds of sounds can you make?

Make three short high sounds.
Make three longer low sounds.

Play a sound pattern.
Play it again, think it and play it again.
Try to play it backwards.

Sound Frame

Provide a coat rack, games rack or stable old book stand capable of holding several suspended objects within reach.

Ask the children to bring anything that makes a sound which can be tied to the frame, e.g.

Dustbin lids,
Suspended nails,
Tin pans from weighing scales,
Different lengths and width of tubing—copper or plastic,
Tin mugs,
Plant pots graded in size and sound,
Chain belts,
Old bicycle chains,
Milk bottle tops,
Parts of old engines and bicycle wheels etc.
A selection of beaters should be readily available.
All these could be used for experiments with sounds. (Chap. 2, pp. 36–38.)

Recognition and exploration of conventional instruments

It would be ideal to provide as many of these as possible: drums, triangles of various sizes, piano, violin, recorder, Indian bells, tambourine.

Flash cards matching pictures to instruments and then cards showing the names of instruments which can be matched to the instruments are one way in which "musical instrument" games can be introduced. Very young children respond readily to these games.

Cards for older children may be developed as follows:

173

13.

Find a triangle

What sounds can you make?

Tell your teacher or write
down which words the
sounds make you think of.

Make up a rhythm for the triangle

CARD 13

A poem could be written about a triangle (Chap. 6, p. 128) or a triangle sound could be incorporated in a story (Chap. 2, p. 24). The children could be asked to choose a tambourine and find a friend and play rhythms to each other, i.e.

"Ask your friend to imitate it—was it just like yours?"

"Have a musical conversation with your friend just by using your instrument. Be happy, angry or sad."

Another variation could be to ask the children to find instruments which could make these sounds (Chap. 6, p. 118):

Children laughing
Birds singing
Wind blowing
Waves splashing

Do they know any more?

Sounds of animals,
Sounds which make them happy,
Sounds which make them sad.

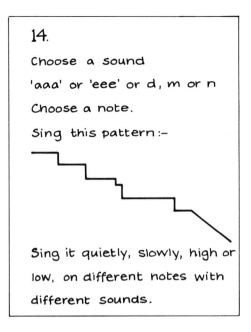

14.

Choose a sound

'aaa' or 'eee' or d, m or n

Choose a note.

Sing this pattern :-

Sing it quietly, slowly, high or low, on different notes with different sounds.

CARD 14

Is there a piano in your school?

Examine the mechanics of the piano. Remove the cover. Make sure the piano is treated carefully. Play a note on the piano then play another note. Ask the children if it is higher or lower than the first note you played. Now see if they can sing the note you played. Can they find the note on another instrument, i.e. Glockenspiel, Recorder or Violin? Ask them to sing a high note, then a low note. Sing all the notes between the high note and low note. Sing a high note to "ah"—sing quickly. Sing slowly. Later sing a pattern. (Chap. 4, p. 75.)

```
┌─────────────────────────────────────┐
│  15.                                 │
│                                      │
│  Sing up to a high note.             │
│                                      │
│  Sing down to a low note.            │
│                                      │
│  Make your body move up with         │
│                                      │
│  your voice.                         │
│                                      │
│  Make your body move down with       │
│                                      │
│  your voice.                         │
│                                      │
│  Make these sounds and move to them  │
│                                      │
│  A quick sound.                      │
│                                      │
│  A slow heavy sound.                 │
│                                      │
│  Draw patterns of your sounds        │
│                                      │
│  and movements.                      │
└─────────────────────────────────────┘
```

CARD 15

Sounds related to different levels and speed of bodily movements.

An extension of the work on this card could be children working in pairs and listening to each other's sounds, choosing opposite sounds, i.e. high or low, making their sounds and moving together at different levels. (Chap. 5, p. 108.) Valuable language development follows discussion of the sounds and movements.

Introduction to treble stave

CARD 16

Flash cards such as these are invaluable both as preparation for sol-fa and for consolidating rhythm recognition. Children could

be asked to clap or tap on an instrument rhythms of this kind:

Rhythms could be related to a child's name. (Chap. 2, p. 32.)

Jennifer   John   Mary

Later, more advanced children could be encouraged to sing in sol-fa, where the teacher sings, for example, "Doh, me" in any key and asks them to find the interval on a glockenspiel or piano.

It can be helpful to give the correct name of the note on the reverse side of the card:

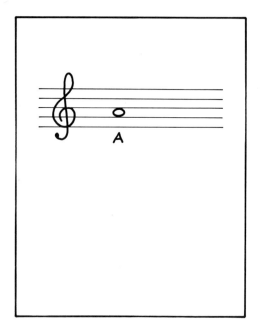

These suggestions are from ideas which have worked for us, and which have helped busy teachers to encourage the children to extend their experiments in the classroom.

Bibliography

Some books which we have found useful

R. Addison, *Children Make Music*, Holmes McDougall Ltd., 1967.

P. Armitstead, *English in the Middle Years*, Basil Blackwell, 1972.

T. Bachmann and R. P. Getz, *Songs to Read*, The Continental Press Inc., Elizabethtown, 1970.

M. Berry, *Music Makers*, Stages 1, 2 and 3, Longmans, 1968.

H. Borten, *Do You Hear What I Hear?*, Abelard-Schuman, New York, 1960.

M. Brearley (Ed.), *Fundamentals in the First School*, Basil Blackwell, 1969.

B. Britten and I. Holst, *The Wonderful World of Music*, Macdonald, 1958.

W. McD. Cameron and M. Cameron, *Education in Movement in the Infant School*, Basil Blackwell, 1969.

G. Carter, *Discovering Music*, Book 1: *How It Began*, Book 2: *Craftsmen of Music*, Book 3: *How It Is Written*, Ginn, 1966.

K. Cox, *Music For Me*, Book 1: *Melody*, Book 2: *Pattern*, Book 3: *Rhythm*, and a Teacher's Guide. University of London Press, 1968.

J. Cutforth, *English in the Primary School*, Basil Blackwell, 1951.

J. Darlow, *Musical Instruments*, A. and C. Black Ltd., 1968.

J. Dean, *Reading, Writing and Talking*, A. and C. Black Ltd., 1968.

R. Noble, *Folk Tunes to Accompany*, Novello.

W. de la Mare, *Collected Rhymes and Verses*, Faber, 1944.

Department of Education and Science, *Movement—physical education in the primary years*, H.M.S.O., 1972.

J. Dixon, *Growth through English*, O.U.P., 1967.

P. Gammond, *The Meaning and Magic of Music*, Paul Hamlyn, 1970.

B. Harrop, *Carol, gaily carol. Christmas songs for children*, A. and C. Black Ltd., 1973.

179

C. Hodgetts, *Sing True. A collection of songs and hymns for use in School assembly*, with a Piano edition, The Religious Educational Press Ltd., 1969.

Inner London Education Authority, *Movement Education for Infants*, 1963.

B. Ireson, *The Young Puffin Book of Verse*, Puffin, 1970.

A. Jones and J. Mulford, *Children Using Language*, Oxford University Press, 1971.

R. Laban, *Modern Educational Dance*, Second edition revised by L. Ullmann, Macdonald and Evans, 1963.

E. Lawrence, *The Origins and Growth of Modern Education*, Penguin, 1970.

S. Marshall, *An Experiment in Education*, O.U.P.

R. E. Masters, *Sounds and the Orchestra*, Macmillan, 1967.

D. Maxwell-Timmins, *Music is Fun*, Parts 1 and 2, and a teacher's handbook, Schofield and Sims Ltd., 1969.

B. Maybury, *Wordscapes*, Oxford University Press, 1973.

S. Milligan, *Silly Verse for Kids*, Puffin, 1968.

Music in Action, Book 1: *The Sound of the Sea*, Book 2: *The Sound of the City*, Book 3: *The Sound of the Country*, Rupert Hart-Davis Educational Publications, 1968.

J. Paynter and P. Aston, *Sound and Silence*, Cambridge University Press, 1970.

J. Paynter, *Hear and Now, an introduction to modern music in schools*, Universal edition, 1972.

G. Reynolds, *A Child's Book of Composers*, Novello and Co. Ltd., 1963.

M. E. Rose, *The Morning Cockerel Book of Readings*, with a Book of Accompaniments, Rupert Hart-Davis Educational Publications, 1967.

J. Russell, *Creative Dance in the Primary School*, Macdonald and Evans, 1965.

George Self, *New Sounds in Class*, Universal edition.

S. Walker, *Rondes et Chansons*, F. Warne and Co. Ltd., 1968.

L. F. Wood and L. B. Scott, *Singing Fun*, George Harrap and Co. Ltd., 1962.

The Young Reader's Guides to Music, Oxford University Press, 1960. There are such titles as "The Sorcerer's Apprentice and Other Stories", "The Orchestra", "Great Performers", "Boyhoods of Great Composers".

Index